T0222396

JavaScript for Web Developers

Understanding the Basics

Mark Simon

Apress®

JavaScript for Web Developers: Understanding the Basics

Mark Simon
Ivanhoe, VIC, Australia

ISBN-13 (pbk): 978-1-4842-9773-5   ISBN-13 (electronic): 978-1-4842-9774-2
https://doi.org/10.1007/978-1-4842-9774-2

Managing Director, Apress Media LLC: Welmoed Spahr
Acquisitions Editor: Smriti Srivastava
Development Editor: Laura Berendson
Coordinating Editor: Mark Powers

Cover designed by eStudioCalamar

Cover image designed by Freepik (www.freepik.com)

Distributed to the book trade worldwide by Apress Media, LLC, 1 New York Plaza, New York, NY 10004, U.S.A. Phone 1-800-SPRINGER, fax (201) 348-4505, e-mail orders-ny@springer-sbm.com, or visit www.springeronline.com. Apress Media, LLC is a California LLC and the sole member (owner) is Springer Science + Business Media Finance Inc (SSBM Finance Inc). SSBM Finance Inc is a **Delaware** corporation.

For information on translations, please e-mail booktranslations@springernature.com; for reprint, paperback, or audio rights, please e-mail bookpermissions@springernature.com.

Apress titles may be purchased in bulk for academic, corporate, or promotional use. eBook versions and licenses are also available for most titles. For more information, reference our Print and eBook Bulk Sales web page at http://www.apress.com/bulk-sales.

Any source code or other supplementary material referenced by the author in this book is available to readers on GitHub (https://github.com/Apress/JavaScript-for-Web-Developers). For more detailed information, please visit https://www.apress.com/gp/services/source-code.

Paper in this product is recyclable.

To my parents. Long since passed on, but still there whenever I ask a question or make a silly remark.

Table of Contents

TABLE OF CONTENTS

About the Author

Mark Simon has been involved in training and education since the beginning of his career. He started as a teacher of mathematics but soon moved into IT consultancy and training because computers are much easier to work with than high school students! He has worked with and trained in several programming and coding languages and currently focuses on web development and database languages. When not involved in work, you will generally find Mark listening to or playing music, reading, or just wandering about.

About the Technical Reviewer

Jeff Friesen is a freelance software developer and educator conversant in multiple operating systems, programming languages, and other technologies. His specialty is Java Standard Edition.

He is currently exploring bare metal programming for the Raspberry Pi and also exploring machine learning. He's also developing his own programming languages and tools (such as compilers and a news aggregator) that facilitate his life.

Introduction

For the impatient:

If you're anxious to get going, you can ignore all of this and skip over to the **Setup** section. It's very important and will make the rest of the book much easier to work with.

When you load a web page, it's quite possible that you'll see the result of up to five technologies. Two of these will have occurred at the web server, and three will be happening within the browser itself.

On the server, the page and its components may well have been generated by software. Typically, though not necessarily, that software may be something like PHP, which is a scripting language. In turn, the software may access a database to get some of its data using a database language called SQL.

The eventual output will be in the form of HTML. That HTML will be sent back to the browser.

The browser will then begin processing the HTML. If there's a reference to additional images, the browser will request these and use them when they arrive. The HTML is also likely to include references to CSS and JavaScript files. The three important browser technologies involved are as follows:

- HTML: This is the language that defines the **content** of the page. By itself, it's given a basic appearance by the browser, but the appearance is probably enhanced by CSS.

- CSS: This is the language that defines the **presentation** of the page. This includes colors, text properties, layout, and some visual effects. CSS has grown dramatically over the years and has become very sophisticated. It even includes some simple animation.

- JavaScript: This is the language that defines the **behavior** of the page. Most of what isn't static is controlled by JavaScript. HTML does include some interaction with the user, such as with web forms, but JavaScript can make the whole page interactive.

This book is, of course, about JavaScript.

It's best to read this book with your computer in front of you so that you can get your hands on all of the concepts. As you do so, you'll develop a good understanding of what JavaScript does and how to make it happen.

To begin with, Chapter 1 will take you through some basic concepts of JavaScript and show you how to use the browser's built-in developer tools to experiment with them. Chapter 2 will take you through a simple game to apply some of these concepts, as well as a few new ones.

An important part of using JavaScript will be working with the web page itself, and Chapter 3 will take you through the ideas, followed by Chapter 4, which builds a slide show project to put these ideas into practice.

Many websites include a form for the user to work with. Chapter 5 will show you how to work with web forms, and Chapter 6 will build a simple special purpose calculator using JavaScript and a form.

Chapter 7 will focus on seeing how JavaScript can work with CSS and will also look at event listeners, which are the basic interface between JavaScript and user actions. We'll then go on to use that to show and hide content and generate a pop-up image gallery in Chapters 8 and 9.

Finally, in Chapter 10, we'll have a look at Ajax, which allows JavaScript to communicate with a web server to get additional resources.

What happens next is, of course, up to you. With what you'll learn in this book, you'll be ready to create your own interactive web pages and to rework any web projects which you may have inherited.

A Little Bit of History

The early World Wide Web was pretty static, which might have been boring if everything wasn't so new. By static, we mean that once you load a page, all that was left was to look at it and click on a link to load the next page.

In 1995, Netscape, a company that developed the most significant graphical web browser at the time, decided to liven things up by adding a scripting language to the browser. This would make the page more interactive and would be capable of changing the content of the page dynamically.

Netscape considered embedding the Java language, which was a newish language and environment that was starting to become fashionable, but decided on creating their own language, under the guidance of Brendan Eich. Even so, Java became popular in the form of plug-ins and "applets" and is still used in some other environments.

The browser scripting language was to be based on another language called Scheme and would be called LiveScript. However, due to Java's popularity at the time, the syntax was designed to look like Java, and the language was renamed as JavaScript, which has been a source of confusion ever since. JavaScript and Java are simply not the same language, even though there's a superficial resemblance both in name and syntax.

Microsoft, not wishing to be left out, added a clone of JavaScript, called JScript, to their new browser called Internet Explorer.[1] However, it was never quite the same. As the browsers developed, so too did the

---

[1] Microsoft also decided to add VBScript to Internet Explorer under the impression the developers actually wanted to write code in Visual Basic. That's all in the past now.

differences between them. In 1996, Netscape submitted JavaScript to ECMA for standardization.

Microsoft went on to dominate the Web, at the same time resisting efforts at standardization. In 2004, Mozilla, the reincarnation of Netscape, released Firefox, which started to loosen Microsoft's stranglehold on the Web, and the push to JavaScript standardization was intensified. Google released Chrome in 2008, and now JavaScript was gaining strength.

What was originally just JavaScript has become known as ECMAScript, and it is now a language that can be used in environments other than a web browser. When used in a web browser, it's still referred to as JavaScript.

ECMAScript, and JavaScript with it, have gone through some serious language improvements over the years. Today, it's a mature language with many sophisticated programming features.

Organization of the Book

Every bit of JavaScript you'll learn about is useful, and every example you see is just that – an example. Some of the examples are more realistic than others.

This book has two main types of chapters:

- Some chapters focus purely on learning a new set of skills. You're encouraged to participate in front of your computer and experiment as you go.

- Some chapters work on projects. There'll be a little bit of experimenting to explain a few points, but they're mostly aimed at writing a coherent script that does something useful.

In some cases, you'll write some code that you can save in a code library to reuse in other projects.

Older Methods

There have been *many* improvements to the way JavaScript works, especially over recent years. However, each browser vendor will implement these improvements in their own time, and each user will update their browser in their own time. As a result, writing JavaScript for the Web is a balance of using techniques that are as modern as possible, without at the same time leaving too many users behind.

Thankfully, modern browsers have gone past the sorts of major discrepancies that have been the bane of web developers for so many years. They're all more or less compatible with the latest mainstream web technologies, and they're mostly on the path to acceptable standards.

In this book, all of the JavaScript code will work on all the major browsers, even if those browsers are a few years old. If you want to check on a particular feature, you can check one of the following sites:

- Can I Use: `https://caniuse.com/`

- MDN Web Docs: `https://developer.mozilla.org/en-US/`

In the book, there will be the occasional reference to older ways of doing things. That's not because you'll need them, or to instill a sense of nostalgia. Rather, it's because you may well encounter these techniques in other code, such as any code you're trying to maintain, or samples of code you might stumble across on the Web somewhere.

What You Should Already Know

Web development is about web pages, and JavaScript is one part of that. To really understand what's going on, you should also know something about web pages.

Of course, we'll assume that you've spent some time on the Web and you know about using forms and clicking on links.

From a technical point of view, you should also know about HTML. You don't need to be an expert, and we'll cover some details in the book when dealing with specific applications. But you should know a little about how HTML works.

Much of the visual work is done with CSS. That's the style sheet language for web pages, and you should know a little about that too. Again, you don't need to be an expert, but it's good to have an idea of what it is and how it's used. Anything tricky will be covered in specific applications.

If you know anything about programming in another language, such as C++, or Python, or PHP, or Java, or dozens of other languages, then you'll already have some of the theory covered.

However, remember that each programming language is different, so you don't want to be caught out by expecting the new language to do things exactly the same way as other languages. It would be a mistake to develop an attitude that this language *should* do things the same way as the other.

Setup

If you've planned a holiday near the beach somewhere, you may decide to take this book with you for a little light reading. Hopefully it's not too hard to read.

However, you'll get more from this book if you follow along with the worked samples. To get the most out of this book, you'll need

- A copy of the sample website to work on

- A decent coding editor

- If possible, a web server of some sort

Here are the details.

The Sample Site

In this book, we'll be working on a sample website. There's nothing fancy in the site – it's just a collection of JavaScript samples and projects.

You can look at a live version of the site at `https://pure-javascript.net`.

You should download your own copy of the sample site from `https://github.com/Apress/JavaScript-for-Web-Developers`

This is essentially the same as the live sample, except that the actual JavaScript is empty. Filling in the JavaScript is what this book is all about.

Unzip the file and put the sample folder in a convenient location.

A Coding Editor

Apart from images, most of the files for a website, especially the sample site here, are text files. That means you can edit these files with any old text editor, even Windows Notepad, if that's your idea of having a good time.

More realistically, you'll want to use a text editor designed for writing code. Here are the features you'll want:

- There is a view of the project folder, making it easy to switch between files.

- The coding editor supports **syntax highlighting**, which recognizes the type of document you're editing (HTML, CSS, JavaScript, etc.) and highlights the parts of the language.

You may already have your preferred coding editor. If you don't, you can try one of these:

- Pulsar: `https://pulsar-edit.dev/`

  This is the successor to the Atom Text Editor.

- VSCodium: `https://vscodium.com/`

  This is the open source of Microsoft's Visual Studio Code (`https://code.visualstudio.com/`), without Microsoft's specific telemetry and proprietary features.

Both are free, cross-platform, and open source. They also have additional extension packages available to customize your editor.

Running a Web Server

You can, in principle, open a file with JavaScript in your browser, and it might even work. However, modern browsers are getting more and more paranoid about running local JavaScript scripts.

You'll get most out of this book if you can run your code through a web server, and it's surprisingly easy to get one going.

If you're doing a lot of web development, you may already have a web server installed on your development machine, such as XAMPP or MAMP. They're pretty full-on and include database software and server scripting with PHP. You don't need so much if you're just developing HTML, CSS, or JavaScript.

There are many ways of running a much lighter web server. Both Pulsar and VSCodium have add-on packages available to run a simple web server from the coding editor itself.

However, the simplest solution is to download one. You can get one called Micro Web Server from

`https://github.com/manngo/micro-web-server`

It looks like this:

Macintosh	Windows

To set it up:

1. Select the location of your sample folder.

2. Save the project. You can use **Save As ...** to give your project a new name.

3. Check the port number. 8000 is probably OK, but 8080 is a common alternative.

4. Start.

When the server is started, you'll see a link to the site, something like
http://localhost:8000
You can click on it to load the page in your browser.

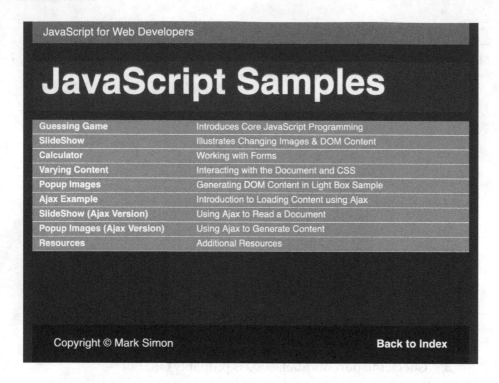

Appendix A has some information on using alternative web servers.

CHAPTER 1

Working with JavaScript

If you're completely new to JavaScript, or to programming altogether, there are some basic concepts that you'll need to know. Many of these concepts are common to other programming languages, but every language has its own twists and quirks.

In this chapter, we'll have an introductory look at the following ideas:

- How you write JavaScript statements

- Working with variables

- Working with different types of basic data

- Functions

- Adding comments to your code

- Special values

Even if you're familiar with these concepts from another language, it's worth glancing over this chapter in case things are significantly different from your own experience.

You'll then have a look at setting up a basic outline for adding JavaScript to your web pages.

© Mark Simon 2023
M. Simon, *JavaScript for Web Developers*, https://doi.org/10.1007/978-1-4842-9774-2_1

In later chapters, of course, we'll have a look at more advanced concepts, such as the following:

- Working with JavaScript control structures in Chapter 2 and further chapters

- Working with HTML elements in Chapters 3 and 4

- Working with forms and data in Chapters 5 and 6

- Interacting with the user and manipulating styles in Chapters 7, 8, and 9

- Working with Ajax in Chapter 10

But first, we'll have a look at how JavaScript works.

Working with the Developer Tools

This chapter is going to be very interactive, so you'll need a very interactive JavaScript tool. Fortunately, most modern browsers have just the tool you need in the Developer Tools.

You'll find the Developer Tools handy not just for this chapter, but for debugging your JavaScript and even your CSS and HTML. You can access the Developer Tools through one of the menus, but you can also use one of these shortcuts:

OS	Keys	Meaning
MacOS	⌥ ⌘ I	option-command-I
Windows	^ ⇧ I	control-shift-I

You'll see something like Figure 1-1.

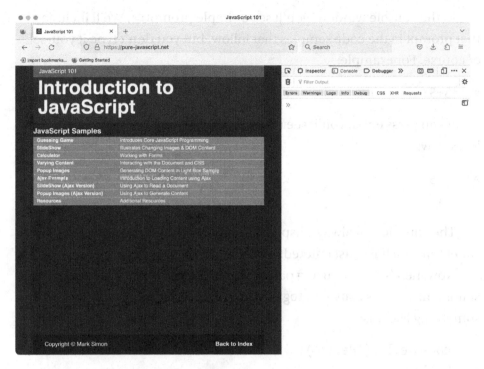

Figure 1-1. *The Developer Tools*

In the figure, the developer toolbox has been docked to the right.

You don't need to have this particular page open: any page will do. Later, however, you'll use the console to work with specific pages.

When using the console, you'll notice a few peculiarities:

- All expressions and values are automatically output whenever you press enter. That is, you won't get a new line, but you will get a value.

- If you want a new line of code, you need to press shift-enter.

Although we'll be using the console interactively, you can also write to the console from your JavaScript. You wouldn't normally see the output, of course, but you can open up the console while you're troubleshooting.

3

In the console window, you'll see a simple prompt: ». We'll include that prompt in the code samples that follow, but you don't type it yourself, of course. For example:

```
»    3+5
```

If you press enter, you'll see the evaluated result after a sort of left arrow:

```
»    3+5
←    8
```

The console will always display the value of the expression or statement you have just entered.

Now, here's the confusing part. Sometimes, you will use a special statement, such as `console.log()`. After you press enter, you'll see something like this:

```
»    console.log('Hello');
     Hello
←    undefined
```

You're actually seeing *two* results here. The first is the *output* of the `console.log()` command: `Hello`, as you would expect. The second is the *value of the statement*, which, for technical reasons, is a special value called `undefined`. If you think that's confusing, well, yes, it is. The good news is that you can ignore it.

In the samples, you'll sometimes also see some additional text after a double-slash (`//`):

```
»    console.log('Hello');    //  print Hello to Console
```

We'll say more on that later, but that text is called a **comment** and is ignored by JavaScript. It's only there for the human reading the code.

Much of the rest of the book deals with real code which you'll write and save in their own documents. However, from time to time, we'll need the console again to experiment with a few ideas. As a reminder, we'll show the prompt character when we do.

For the rest of this chapter, you can press enter after each sample, unless you're asked not to. In some cases, we'll show you what the output should look like, but mostly we'll leave that to you.

Getting Your Hands on JavaScript

Although JavaScript is meant to be written as a script and run later with the web page, the console will give you the chance to use JavaScript more interactively. That means we'll be able to experiment and try out new ideas.

Before that, however, we'll need to go over some basic concepts.

Some Basic Concepts

JavaScript is written in a text file, and it's up to the browser to read, interpret, and run the code. There have been a number of ways to convert text code into runnable code.

- Compiling means interpreting the code and converting it to binary code, which runs natively on the computer.

  Once the compiled code has been saved, it is ready to run. The compiler will also have had the opportunity to look for errors and to find more efficient ways of running the code, a process called optimization. Sometimes, this is also referred to as AOT (Ahead of Time) compiling.

- Interpreting means interpreting the code line by line as it runs the code. It's normally slower as it needs to interpret everything at runtime and often needs to reinterpret the same code later. The interpreter doesn't get the chance to make many optimizations.

  The major benefit of interpreting over compiling is it's easy to write and test code on the fly since we don't have to wait for the code to recompile every time we make a change.

Today, JavaScript uses an in-between method called JIT (Just in Time) compiling. The code is compiled by the browser during runtime, often in sections when the code reaches that point. It allows the convenience of keeping the code in its text form, but running quickly and efficiently.

All programming languages follow a few core principles. These principles include the following:

- Writing JavaScript statements

- Calculation

- Data and variables

- Functions

- Control structures such as testing and repetition

- JavaScript object

In this chapter, we'll cover the first few. We'll look at the others as we start writing more code in later chapters.

Before we start, we'll need to clear up some terminology. JavaScript, like most other programming languages, is very fussy about what you type, so to avoid ambiguity, we'll need to know the correct names for some of the characters:

Characters	Name	Some uses
;	Semicolon	End of a statement
( )	Parentheses	ArithmeticGrouping values
{ }	Braces	Blocks of codeDefining an object (see later)
[ ]	(Square) Brackets	Defining an array (see later)Selecting a member of a collection
` `	Backticks	In JavaScript, it's used for special strings (see later)
|	Vertical bar, a.k.a. "pipe"	Used in logical expressions
&	Ampersand	Used in logical expressions

You'll learn more about using these characters later. This is just to make sure we know what they're called.

Statements

JavaScript is made up of a number of **statements** and statement blocks. There are different types of statements.

The simplest type of JavaScript statement simply calls some predefined block of code:

```
»   console.log('Hello');
```

The console.log command is really a call to a predefined block of code, called the console.log() **function**. In this case, the console.log() function outputs a value to the console. When writing real code later, you can use this function to print values for troubleshooting.

Functions are a fundamental of JavaScript development, and we will be using and creating functions throughout the course.

Statement Blocks

There are times when you need to put multiple statements in a block. Usually it's so that a group of statements can be run or ignored together, possibly after a test. Sometimes, it's just to isolate the statements from the rest of the code.

A block of statements is wrapped inside braces. For example:

»
```
{
    console.log('Hello');
    console.log('Goodbye');
}
```

To get the extra lines in the console log, you may need to use shift-enter.

In this case, grouping the statements has no real effect. Later, it will be an important technique.

You will have noticed that in the code sample, the statements inside the block are indented. JavaScript doesn't care whether the code is indented or not, but the indentation makes it easier to see how the blocks are structured. All of the code in the book will be clearly indented, and it's *strongly* recommended that you do the same to make your code easier to read and maintain.

Expressions

An **expression** is a combination of terms that results in a single value. Examples of expressions are

```
1 + 2
12 / 3
5
```

In the console, all expressions are automatically evaluated and output as soon as you press Enter, so you never need to ask for it. For example:

```
»   3 + 5
←   8
```

Expressions are of no use in themselves. You would normally use them as part of a statement. For example:

```
»   a = 12/3;
»   console.log(a + 5);
    9
←   undefined
```

Adding, dividing, etc., are called **arithmetic operations**, and the symbols are called **arithmetic operators**.

There are other operations, such as boolean and string operations, as well as object operations. We will learn more about these operations after we learn more about data types.

Spacing

You don't normally have to include spaces in your expression. For example:

```
»   console.log(1+2+3);
»   console.log(1 + 2 + 3); //Same thing
```

However, there are times when you need spaces to clear up an ambiguity, such as with the minus sign:

```
»   console.log(1--2);        //  error
»   console.log(1 - -2);      //  1 minus negative 2
    3
```

Semicolons

There is a lot of argument about the use of semicolons in learned circles! In this book, we recommend them.

Classically, JavaScript statements end with a semicolon (;):

```
»    a = 3;
»    console.log(a + 4);
```

JavaScript is forgiving of missing semicolons, if they can be guessed:

```
»    a = 3
»    console.log(a + 4)
```

They can normally be guessed if they would have occurred at the end of the line. This guessing is referred to as *automatic semicolon insertion*.

Semicolons *cannot* be guessed if the semicolon is expected to occur in the middle of the line:

```
»    a = 3 console.log(a + 4)     // error
```

In this case, you have no choice but to separate the statements with a semicolon:

```
»    a = 3; console.log(a + 4)     // works
```

The point is semicolons at the end of a statement are generally optional *if the end of the statement is also the end of the line*, which it normally is.

However, some consider it good practice to always mark the end of a statement with a semicolon anyway.

In this book, all code will include semicolons at the end of every statement.

Variables and Assignment Statements

Variables are a mainstay of all programming languages. Variables are containers of data. They are actually named references to somewhere in memory that will hold the data.

Variables can have simple names, such as x or a, or longer names such as element.

To put a value into a variable, you use an **assignment statement**:

```
[variable] = [expression]
```

This places the value on the right of the equals sign into the variable named on the left. For example:

```
»   a = 3;
```

This places the value 3 into the variable called a.

Although you might read this as "a equals 3", it is better to understand this as "the new value of a is 3", or "a gets 3", or "a becomes 3". For example:

```
»   a = 0;
»   a = 3;
```

The first assignment puts 0 into a. The second statement does not state whether a is 3; just that the new value is 3.

Variables on Both Sides of an Assignment

A JavaScript assignment statement may contain a particular variable on both sides of the equals sign. In this case:

- Variables to the right are parts of an expression: their current (old) value will be used.

- A variable to the left is being assigned a new value.

11

The following statement illustrates this further:

```
»   a = 3;
»   a = a + 1;  //  New value of a gets old value + 1
»   console.log(a);
```

This statement is best read as "the new value of a is the old value of a plus 1". Nobody ever says it this way, but we should at least remember that it's what it means.

Increment and Decrement

It is common to increase or decrease variables by 1. JavaScript uses the increment or decrement operators for this:

```
++a or a++:  increment
--a or a--:  decrement
```

As a statement by itself, it doesn't matter whether you use the **pre-increment** (++a) or the **post-increment** (a++) operator; the same is true for the decrement operators. For example:

```
»   a=3; a++; console.log(a);
»   a=3; ++a; console.log(a);
```

will give you the same results.

However, you can also use the operators in the middle of an expression. In this case, the pre- operators will apply before the value is used, while the post- operators will apply after. For example:

```
»   a=3; console.log(++a); console.log(a);  //  pre-increment
    4
    4
»   a=3; console.log(a++); console.log(a);  //  post-increment
    3
    4
```

In the first case, the variable a will be incremented to 4 *before* it is displayed. In the second case, the variable a will be displayed after, so the console.log() will display the old value of 3. In both cases, the second console.log() will show the new value of 4.

Note that if you're just using the statement by itself, it's common to prefer the post-increment operator for no special reason.

Chaining Assignments

You can chain assignments together in a single statement. A statement such as the following is common:

```
»    a = b = c = 0;
»    console.log(a);
»    console.log(b); // etc
```

Reading from the *right*, this will put 0 into c, which then goes into b, which then goes into a.

Assignment Operators

JavaScript also has combined arithmetic **assignment operators**. These allow you to perform an operation with the old value of a variable and assign it as the new value. They are, in fact, simply an abbreviation for separate operators.

For example:

```
»    value = 2;
»    value = value+3;
```

can be written as:

```
»    value = 2;
»    value += 3;
```

This may not look like much of an improvement, but JavaScript programmers usually prefer the second format, and we will be using it here:

```
»    a = 5;
»    a += 10;
»    console.log(a);
```

Assignment operators include the following:

Operator	Meaning
+=	Add to old value
-=	Subtract from old value
*=	Multiply old value by
/=	Divide old value by
%=	Old value remainder …
+=	Concatenate to old value

The last operation of concatenation means joining strings and is very common among JavaScript programmers. You'll look at concatenation later in this chapter.

We now have three ways of incrementing a variable by 1. They are

```
»    a = a+1;
»    a += 1;
»    a++;
```

in increasing order of preference.

The Naming of Variables

Out of pure laziness, we've used a single letter variable a. As we said earlier, variable names can be (much) longer. JavaScript variables must follow a number of rules. The main rules are as follows:

1. Variables must be single words (no spaces). If you need to use multiple words, you can **camelCase** (join them with a capital letter at the beginning of each new word) them.

    For example: `familyName`

2. Variables must start with a letter but may also contain numerals, as long as they don't start with one. Most JavaScript programmers use a lowercase letter at the beginning.

    For example: `big2small`

3. Variables should not contain special characters, except the underscore (_). You can use one or two other special characters, but it is not common practice to use them.

    For example: `part_one` (However, most JavaScript programmers would use `partOne` instead.)

The other major rule when naming JavaScript variables is that you shouldn't use names that are reserved as part of the JavaScript language. This does not rule out names of preexisting functions or variables, which you are at liberty of replacing (sometimes at your peril).

Case Sensitivity

JavaScript variables, together with the rest of the JavaScript language, are case sensitive. This means that you cannot define them in one case and use them in another. For example:

```
»    thing = 'Hello';
»    console.log(Thing); //  oops
```

The `console.log()` function will attempt to display the contents of the `Thing` variable. However, this was not defined in the previous statement, which allocates a value to the `thing` (lowercase) variable. Thus you can, if you like, have 32 (2^5) variables which you spell the same way as `thing`. This can be a source of confusion if you are not careful.

Declaring Variables

It's one thing to use and assign variables. JavaScript first has to become aware of the variables you're going to use so that it can prepare storage for them. When you prepare for a variable, you are **declaring** the variable.

In JavaScript, there are *four* ways to declare a variable:

- Traditionally, you can declare them in a `var` statement.

The console output may be a little confusing here. The output of a `var` statement is `undefined`. It doesn't mean that it didn't work – just that there's no output value. On the other hand, the output of an *assignment* is the value you have just assigned. That's why you can chain them.

Modern JavaScript has two alternatives to `var`:

- The let statement is similar to var, but it has some important differences, which we'll talk about.

  ```
  »    let a;
  »    a = 3;
  ```

- The const statement lets you declare a constant. A constant can only be set once, so it's more stable.

  »   const a = 3;
  »   a = 4; // error

Notice that the const statement assigns the value at the same time. You have to do it this way, since a const can't be assigned later.

You can also do this with var and let:

»   var a = 3;
»   let a = 3;

The fourth method is a legacy method:

- A variable may be automatically declared when you assign a value to a new variable. For example:

  »   b = 3;   // creates a new variable

That last method is what we've been doing all along so far, but it's going to have to stop now. We'll see why shortly.

You can declare multiple variables with a single statement. For example:

»   var a = 3, b = 4;

From JavaScript's perspective, it makes no difference whether you use a single statement or multiple statements. Using a single statement, however, might be handy if you're trying to visually group the new variables.

In the Firefox console in particular, you can't redeclare any variables defined with either `let` or `const`, which might cramp your style. If you need to redeclare them, you should reload your page and start again.

Remember that in real JavaScript, you can't redeclare `let` or `const` variables either.

The Difference Between Variable Declaration Types

Modern JavaScript prefers `let` and `const` over `var`.

- The `let` statement is preferable for normal variables, as its behavior is more what you'd expect.

  The problem with `var` is that you can declare it multiple times, and you can declare it *after* you first assign it. The `let` statement won't let you do any of that.

  As well as that, `let` variables are limited in scope to their containing blocks. We'll see more about scope later, but it's to do with how far away the variable is still valid.

- The `const` statement is preferable if you want to make sure that it doesn't (accidentally) change in value. In fact, they are not variable at all and are called **constants**, for the obvious reason.

  Older JavaScript didn't have anything like this, so you just had to use a variable and be careful.

When we write our JavaScript more seriously, we'll use `let` or `const` as needed.

Variables in the Console

In this chapter, which is all done in the console, we're doing things a little differently.

First, as a gentle introduction to variables, we didn't bother declaring them first. From here on, we will. In the next section, "Strict Mode," we'll see how to disallow assigning a variable without declaring it and why we should do that.

Second, the `let` statement can't be used twice for a variable. In some of our examples, we will start from scratch and redeclare our variables as if it's the first time. For that reason, we'll use `var` statements, which will let us get away with it. In later projects, we'll prefer the `let` statement.

The use of declaration statements will be essential when writing functions, where it will be possible to declare variables with the same name, but different data. However, it is good practice *always* to declare variables this way, and this is what we will be doing throughout.

Strict Mode

Modern versions of JavaScript allow an optional **strict mode**, which will help to reduce errors in your code. The most significant change is that it will disallow creating new variables without declaring first.

Why would that be useful? JavaScript's relaxed attitude to declaring variables can get you into trouble. For example:

```
»    value = 5;
»    Value = value + 2;
»    console.log(value);
```

In this example, the second variable is different to the first, since it starts with a capital letter. It will be automatically created, however. This simple typing error can result in some difficult errors to trace.

To enable strict mode, the script must include the following string as the first statement:

```
'use strict';
```

This statement can appear after blank or comment lines but will not work if it is placed after another JavaScript statement.

> The JavaScript console will probably ignore the use strict statement, so we won't bother with it here. Later, when writing real code, we'll definitely be using it.

Comments

JavaScript allows you to insert comments into the text. Comments are text that will not be interpreted by the JavaScript interpreter.

Comments are used for the following reasons:

- To add information that may be of relevance to the developer (or whoever reads the code)

- To disable lines of code without actually deleting them

The second reason is useful in the development process when you want to disable code temporarily.

JavaScript supports two types of comment:

- `// Single Line Comments`

  The // indicates that the remainder of the line is to be treated as a comment. You can use this for a whole line, or the last part of a line.

- `/* Block Style Comments */`

  This allows you to mark a block of several lines as a comment. Alternatively, you can mark out part of a line as a comment.

For example:

```
/*  The following code does something or other.
    It was written by me. Enjoy ... */
console.log('hello');    //  Prints out a message
//  The following code does some more:
console.log('goodbye');
//  The following line has been disabled:
//  console.log('Hello');
```

Note that comments *inside* JavaScript strings will simply be treated as part of the text:

» `console.log('This is /*not*/ a comment!');`

Comments can be used for any purpose at all. Previously you see three very common uses:

- A comment can be used to explain something.

- You can (temporarily) disable a line of code as a comment. This is called **commenting the code out**.

- Comment blocks are often used as headings or to introduce code.

It's also a good idea to include a comment block at the beginning of your JavaScript file to explain what is happening in the file.

Nested Comments

You cannot nest blocked comments; that is, you cannot place one block comment inside another. This is because the second block start will be ignored and the first block end will terminate the comment.

For example:

```
/*  This will not work properly:
    /*  This is not really a nested block */
This line will not be ignored! */
```

However, it is quite OK to have single line comments inside block comments or other single line comments.

Data Types

Partly for historical reasons, partly for efficiency reasons, and partly for other reasons, programming languages generally distinguish between types of data. In JavaScript, there are three basic types:

- Numbers.

- Strings, which means strings of characters. That includes text.

- Boolean, which is one of two values, `true` and `false`, used in logical calculations.

JavaScript refers to these as **primitive** types, not because they've been around for a while, but because they are the most basic. These types of data are sometimes also called scalar. The point is they represent single values.

In addition to that, there are a few special data values which we'll look at later.

The rest, which is what you'll be dealing with very much in JavaScript, is in the form of **objects**. An object is a package. Again, we'll see more on this later.

For now, we'll look at the primitive types.

Numbers

Numbers are one of the fundamental data types in JavaScript. Many languages distinguish between different types of numbers, such as integers and floating-point (decimals), but JavaScript dispenses with the difference and treats all numbers the same.

This does lead to a notorious quirk:

»   `console.log(0.1 + 0.2);`
     `0.30000000000000004`

This is due to internal roundoff error. Such roundoff errors do occur in all computer languages, but most other languages take pains to hide the error, or to offer alternative ways of handling decimals.

Writing Numbers

Numbers can be written with or without decimals:

»   `3`
»   `3.0`
»   `25.4`

They can also be written in a type of Exponential Notation:

»   `1.2345e2     //  =1.2345 × 10²`
←   `123.45`

If you wish, you can use integers in some other bases:

- Binary numbers (base 2) are written with 0b at the beginning, such as 0b101010.

- Octal numbers (base 8) are written with 0o (that's zero followed by the letter o) at the beginning as in 0o52. Historically, they have been written with just a zero at the beginning (052), but that's discouraged because it's ambiguous.

- Hexadecimal numbers (base 16) are written with 0x at the beginning as in 0x2a.

Here are different ways of writing the same number:

```
»   console.log(42, 0x2a, 0o52, 0b101010);
    42 42 42 42
```

Even though you may have entered a number in another notation, JavaScript will generally revert to the standard base 10 form.

Arithmetic

JavaScript will perform arithmetic using the standard rules. Generally this uses values and operations.

The main arithmetic operators are the following:

Symbol	Operation
+	Addition
-	Subtraction
*	Multiplication ($\times$)
/	Division ($\div$)
%	Remainder

JavaScript follows the standard rules of arithmetic. You would have learned about them at school, but we'll go over them again just in case you know someone who's forgotten them.

Associativity

Consider the following expression:

»   12 - 3 + 4

If you were tempted to perform the second operation first, giving you 12-7 or 5, you would be wrong. JavaScript will evaluate this expression from left to right, giving you 9+4 or 13.

However, the rule of associativity only applies when the operators have the same precedence.

Precedence

Consider the following expression:

»   1 + 2 * 3

This will result in 7, as JavaScript observes the convention of multiplying before adding. If you wanted to do the addition first, you would need to put that part of the expression inside parentheses: (1 + 2) * 3. This would then result in 9.

In general, JavaScript follows this order of precedence:

1. (...)

2. * or /

3. + or −

If you have multiple operations at the same precedence, the operations are performed from left to right. Many people only partially understand this rule. Don't be trapped by the following:

```
»    12 / 2 * 3
```

In this case, both operations (/ and *) are on the same level of precedence, so you will perform the division before the multiplication, giving 18 and not 2, which is what you get if you wrongly perform the multiplication first.

Remainder (%)

Sometimes, when you divide two integers (whole numbers), you don't want the whole result. Sometimes, what you want is the **remainder**. The operator is written as a percent sign (%). For example:

```
»    100 % 7;
```

will give you the remainder after dividing 100 by 7 (2).

Now, this may seem a pretty odd sort of thing to ask for, but it is very useful when working with numbers involved in cyclic patterns.

For example, in 100 days, the day of the week will be 2 days ahead of today, since it doesn't matter how may weeks are involved (dividing by 7), but how many days remain after that.

Cyclic values are quite common. For example, what time will it be 100 hours from now?

```
»    h = 14  // 2:00 pm in 24 hour format
»    h = (h + 100) % 24;
»    console.log(h);
```

Because the remainder after division is always a number between 0 and 1 less than the divisor, you may have to zero-base your values. For example, though months are normally numbered from 1 to 12, you should number them from 0 to 11 to do the modulus arithmetic. You can add 1 to the result afterward.

Notice that we've put the expression h + 100 in parentheses. That's because the remainder operation has the same precedence as multiplication and division, which is higher than addition.

You'll very often see this referred to as the Modulus operator. That's not technically correct, as there's a subtle difference between modulus and remainder when it comes to negative numbers. We'll stick to the more correct remainder.

Strings

Strings are containers of text and other characters. That is, they are strings of characters. JavaScript has a few simple string operations available for working with strings as well as a rich collection of functions that can manipulate strings. There are also functions that deal with converting between strings and numbers.

Strings may or may not mean something to the reader:

```
'qwerty'
'Hello'
'23'
```

Note the last expression. It *looks* like number, but it isn't: it's stored differently and will be treated differently when the time comes. However, JavaScript may well convert it to a number if the situation calls for it.

String Literals

A **string literal** is part of the code that defines a string. The distinction may be subtle, but it is important.

27

Suppose you have the following code:

```
»   message = 'Hello';
```

The string literal `'Hello'` defines the string `Hello` that is stored in the variable `message`. The string itself doesn't include the quotes that were used to define the string. The quotes, however, are written so that JavaScript won't confuse the string literal with some other code.

JavaScript allows you to use single or double quotes for string literals, as long as you finish the way you started:

```
'Hello'
"Hello"
```

Sometimes, the choice is affected by the contents of the string:

```
»   console.log('<img src="thing.jpg">');
```

Here, the single quote is used to allow double quotes in the string.

Some users use double quotes to allow single quotes to be used as apostrophes:

```
»   console.log("Don't Worry");
```

If you can, it's better to use proper typographical apostrophes, which don't compete with the code:

```
»   console.log("Don't Worry");
»   console.log('Don't Worry');
```

You can insert a typographical apostrophe using shift-opt-] on the Macintosh or alt-0146 on Windows.

This book prefers single quotes, since it simplifies interacting with HTML, which prefers double quotes for attributes.

One thing to be careful about is that JavaScript *does not use* either single or double typographic quotes to define a string:

```
»    var a = "hello";    --  definitely no go
```

This makes typographic quotes perfectly safe to use inside a string.

The JavaScript console appears to have a preference for double quotes. Whenever it needs to tell you that you have a string, by putting the string in quotes, it will use double quotes. For example:

```
»    'hello'
←    "hello"
```

We'll still use single quotes, though.

Empty Strings

An empty string is a zero-length string with no characters:

```
»    var a = '';
»    var a = "";
```

An empty string can be used to initialize a variable that will be added to later.

Note that an empty string literal can be visually confusing, especially if the font is not monospaced.

Unicode

JavaScript strings are encoded internally in Unicode, specifically UTF-16.

From a practical point of view, that means that a JavaScript string can include any character from any language in the world. It also means that a string usually uses 2 bytes per character, though some characters will take more. None of that affects our normal use of strings.

Strings Are Immutable

Although you can change the value of a string variable, you cannot change the string itself. Any changes to the string require creating a new string and disposing of the old. For example:

```
»    var a = 'Wilma';
»    a = 'Betty';
```

This requires creating a new string for the variable a and disposing of the old one. This happens automatically, so we don't normally need to bother about it. However, it does mean that string operations do a lot of work in the background and so are regarded as expensive.

Escaped Characters

Sometimes, a string literal is supposed to include awkward characters, such as the quote characters or special characters. To allow special characters, the **backslash** character (\) is used as the so-called **escape character**. For example:

```
»    console.log('He said "Don\'t Worry"');
```

Here, the escape sequence \' is used to embed the single quote that would otherwise prematurely terminate the string. (Of course, using a typographical apostrophe would also have avoided the problem altogether.)

Note that the backslash is not actually part of the string. It is simply used to modify the next character. If you really wanted a backslash, you would need to escape it as well:

```
»    console.log('This is a backslash: \\');
```

The escape character can also be used to insert a few special characters such as the tab (\t) or new line (\n):

```
»   console.log('Fruit:\tApple\nColour:\tRed');
←   Fruit:  Apple
    Colour: Red
```

Template Literals

JavaScript *strings* can contain any character at all, but *string literals* have limitations. In particular, you can't include line breaks. For example, this would generate an error:

```
»   var message = 'Hello there.
    Enjoy today';    // error
```

Normally, you would work around this either by including the escaped line break (\n):

```
»   var message = 'Hello there.\nEnjoy today';
```

or by an ugly use of the escape character, which permits a line break without terminating the statement:

```
»   message = 'Hello there.\
»   Enjoy today';
```

Modern versions of JavaScript support **template literals**, which are more flexible than traditional string literals.

One feature is that template literals allow you to embed line breaks:

```
»   message = `Hello there.Enjoy today`;
```

Note that template literals quote strings using the grave character, the so-called backtick (`).

31

A second feature of template literals is that you can include expressions:

```
» var price = 3;
» var quantity = 4;
» console.log(`Total: ${price*quantity}`);
```

Any expression inside the special code ${ } will be evaluated as it would have been outside the string.

String Concatenation

In JavaScript, there is only one direct operation with strings: concatenation. This will join them together.

JavaScript uses the addition sign (+) for concatenation, which is a potential source of error, as we'll see later.

Examples of concatenation are

```
» var a = 'Hello';
» console.log(a + 'Fred');
```

Note that concatenation does not add any extra spaces. If you want them, you will have to add them yourself:

```
» a = 'Fred'; b = 'Nurkk';
» console.log(a + ' ' + b);
```

The fact that concatenation uses the same symbol as addition can cause some odd results when combining the two operations. For example:

```
» console.log('abc' + 1 + 2); //   abc12
» console.log(1 + 2 + 'abc'); //   3abc
```

This is because JavaScript reads the expression from left to right and interprets the plus sign as it seems appropriate.

If you really wanted to add the numbers first, you would need to group them with parentheses:

```
» console.log('abc' + (1 + 2));
```

Later, we will need some numbers from a form or a dialog box. Since all data will be treated as text, we can run into this problem if we are trying to add to them.

String Properties and Methods

JavaScript strings have a number of properties that contain information about the string. You can access the property using the dot (.) notation. For example:

```
» var a = 'abcdefghijklmnop';
» console.log(a.length);
```

The length property is the number of characters in the string. Sometimes, it's not correct: the length property assumes each Unicode character takes 2 bytes, which is not always true.

You can also do this with a string literal:

```
» console.log('abcdefghijklmnop'.length);
```

Strings also have built-in functions, referred to as methods, to process strings; more specifically, they return a new value generated from the old. For example:

```
» var a = 'Hello';
» console.log(a.toUpperCase());
← HELLO
» console.log(a.toLowerCase());
← hello
```

These methods don't change the original string; they return a new string.

Boolean

Boolean values are either `true` or `false`. (Boolean is named after the mathematician George Boole who pioneered mathematical logic.)

You can assign boolean values directly:

```
»   var ok = false;
```

Often it will be the result of a comparison:

```
»   var a = 3, b = 4;
»   var ok = a > b;
»   console.log(ok);
```

You often use boolean values in the following ways:

```
»   var a = 3, b = 4;
»   var ok = a > b;
»   if (ok) console.log('bigger');
```

Boolean values are often used when you need to test a value to decide what to do next. Two such cases are the `if` statement and the `while` statement. You see a simple example of an `if` statement shown previously.

The `while` statement is an example of **iteration**: repeating a process a number of times. A simple example of the `while` statement is

```
»   var n = 0, finish = 10;
»   while(n<finish) {
        n++;                    //  increment n
        console.log(n);
    }
```

Here, the variable n is initialized to 0. It is then incremented and printed out while the test n<finish holds true. You'll see the numbers 1 to 10 printed out, one per line.

We'll be using the `while` statement later.

Using Boolean

Often, we use a boolean value without realizing it. For example:

```
»   var a = 3, b = 5;
»   if(a>b) console.log('a is bigger');
```

In fact, the expression inside parentheses in the if statement is one whose value must be boolean, or at least can be interpreted as boolean. It would be just as correct to put the result into a boolean variable:

```
a = 3; b = 5;
ok = a>b;
if(ok) alert ('a is bigger');
```

Why would you do this? It would be useful if you need to use the same test again later:

```
a = 3; b = 5;
ok = a>b;
if(ok) alert ('a is bigger');
...
if(ok) ...;
```

We will be looking more at the if structure later.

Changing Data Types

By and large, JavaScript will perform any necessary data type conversions automatically, but only if it can. For example:

```
»   var a = '3';
»   console.log(2 * a);
←   6
```

Since you can only multiply numbers, JavaScript will convert the string '3' to a number.

This isn't always possible. If the string can't be interpreted as a number, then it can't be converted. For example:

```
»    var a = 'hello';
»    console.log(2 * a);
     NaN
```

Note that the result is *not* technically an error. It's a special value. We'll look again at NaN shortly.

Sometimes, JavaScript doesn't feel the need to convert anything, even if it can. For example:

```
»    var a = '3';
»    console.log(2 + a);
←    23
```

will give you a different result. In a sense, JavaScript can "add" strings, which really concatenates them. So it is the 2 which is converted to a string for concatenation.

If you want to force the issue, you can manually convert a string to a number:

```
»    var a = '3';
»    console.log(2 + parseInt(a));
```

will force a conversion of a to an integer (whole number) and then perform the addition.

parseInt( ) and parseFloat( )

Two functions exist for conversion from a string to a number: parseInt() and parseFloat().

The parseInt(string) function converts a string into an integer. This function is forgiving: it will convert as much as it can; if the string also contains characters that cannot be converted, it will stop there. For example:

```
»    var a = parseInt('123abc456');
»    console.log(a);
←    123
```

will result in 123, ignoring the rest.

If the string cannot be converted at all, you will again get a special value of NaN (Not a Number):

```
»    a = parseInt('ha ha');
»    console.log(a);
←    NaN
```

Normally, parseInt() will interpret the text as a base 10 number, but this is not always reliable. If you wish to have the string interpreted as a number in a different base, you can give it the optional base argument. For example:

```
»    a = parseInt('10110110', 2);
»    console.log(a);
←    182
```

will interpret the 10110110 as a binary (base 2) number and return 182.

However, even if you want the base 10, it is most reliable to specify the base as such:

```
»    a = parseInt('0123', 10);
```

The parseFloat() function will also change the string to a number but also allows decimals. However, you cannot use this with other bases.

JavaScript will automatically convert strings to numbers if it can and if it feels the need. However, the automatic conversion is not as forgiving as `parseFloat()` or `parseInt()`.

isNaN()

If you need to test whether a conversion to a number is possible, you can use the `isNaN()` function (is Not a Number), and yes, there are two capital Ns in the name. This function actually tests for *failure* of the conversion. For example:

```
»    var b = '456a';
»    var a = b*1;
»    if (isNaN(a)) console.log('oops');
```

The expression `if(...)  ...` is called a conditional expression. It tests whether something is true and if so moves on to the next part of the statement. You'll see more on this structure in Chapter 2 when we use it in a simple game project.

To test for a number, which is a common requirement, you reverse the result with the not (`!`) operator:

```
»    if (!isNaN(a)) console.log('ok');
```

One surprising feature of NaN is that it is not regarded as equal to itself. This allows an alternative test:

```
»    if (a==a) console.log('ok');
```

The `==` operator tests whether two values are the same. This feature is nifty, but you might end up confusing other coders.

Variables and Data Types

Unlike some other programming languages, JavaScript variables are not restricted to one type of data. In some other languages, you declare not only the name, but the data type, such as an integer or a string.

JavaScript *does* distinguish between different data types. However, the data type is determined by the current value, not any preconceived notions.

For example:

```
»   var a;
»   a = 3;
»   console.log(typeof(a));
    "number"
```

The typeof() function gives the data type of the current value.

If you then change the value to a different type, the typeof() function will give the new type:

```
»   a = 'hello';
»   console.log(typeof(a));
    "string"
```

In the trade, we say that JavaScript is **dynamically typed**. The data type will depend on the current value.

Functions

Functions are another mainstay of any programming language, and we will be using and writing functions throughout the course.

We'll be looking at functions in more depth later. However, for now, we will develop an idea of what they are and how we use them.

A function is a block of code that can be used and reused. Traditionally, you might define a function like this:

```
function twice(number) {
    var value = number * 2;
    return value
}
undefined
```

If you find that the console doesn't let you type in the rest of the code, you may need to press shift-enter to get the extra lines.

Just like the var statement (and let and const), the output of a function declaration is undefined. It doesn't mean that the function is undefined – just that there's no output value from the definition.

This sample function is, of course, trivial, but you can test it this way:

```
var a = 3;
var b = twice(a);
console.log(b);
6
```

- The variable number is called a **parameter** variable. It gets assigned the value you give when you call the function.

- The value a in twice(a) is called the **argument**. It's the value that is sent to the function.

- The return statement at the end of the function does 1½ jobs. First, it provides the result of the function. It also ends the function code, which in this case is unnecessary, since we had reached the end anyway; that second job is more useful if you need to finish before the end of the function block.

When defining or calling a function, the function name always includes a pair of parentheses, even if there are no parameters:

```
» function thing() {
    // ...
  }
```

The code is also always wrapped in braces, even if it's only one line of code.

Void Functions

To begin with, JavaScript doesn't have void functions, so this might be a little misleading. Some other languages do have void functions, sometimes referred to as procedures.

If JavaScript did have void functions, they would be functions that don't return a result. They can still do something useful, such as display a message, but they don't calculate any result to output.

In JavaScript, *all* functions return a result. However, unless you specify otherwise, the result is a special magic value, undefined.

Whenever you see return without a value, it always means return undefined;. Whenever you have a function without a return, there's an implied return undefined at the end.

One function you've already seen that does this is the console.log() function. Whenever you call it, the console shows you the output, which is undefined.

JavaScript Dialog Boxes

JavaScript has three functions that will allow you to communicate with the user with a dialog box.

The `alert()` function shows a message with an OK button to dismiss it. You would use it this way:

```
» alert('This is a message');
  undefined
```

Depending on your browser, it will look something like Figure 1-2.

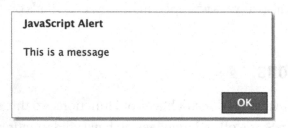

JavaScript Alert

This is a message

OK

Figure 1-2. *JavaScript Alert*

The result of an alert is undefined. This is one of those so-called void functions that aren't really void functions.

The `confirm()` function also displays a message but gives the user a choice of pressing `cancel` or `OK`. To use this, you normally assign a variable to the result of the function, like this:

```
» var response = confirm('You are about to do something
  silly ...');
» console.log(response);
```

Again, depending on your browser, it will look something like Figure 1-3.

> **JavaScript Confirm**
>
> You are about to do something silly ...
>
> cancel   **OK**

Figure 1-3. *JavaScript Confirm*

The result of the function is a boolean value, either `true` or `false`, depending on whether you selected `OK` or `cancel`.

Notice that with both the `alert()` and `confirm()` functions, you have to wait until you responded to the dialog box before you saw the result in the console. That's the feature of these dialog box functions: they all stop everything until the user has dealt with them. We'll see that that's both good and bad.

The `prompt()` also shows a message but allows the user to enter a response in a text box. Again, you need to capture the response in a variable:

```
»    var response = prompt('What is your name?');
»    console.log(response);
```

It looks something like Figure 1-4.

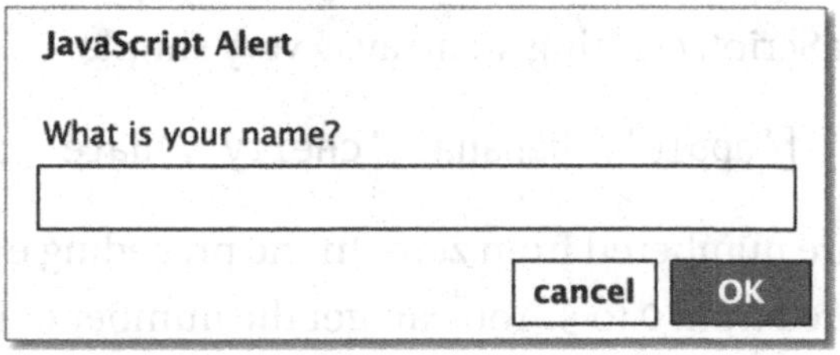

> **JavaScript Alert**
>
> What is your name?
>
> [   ]
>
> cancel   **OK**

Figure 1-4. *JavaScript prompt*

If you click OK, then the result will be whatever text you entered in the text box. If there were no text, the result would be an empty string. If, on the other hand, you click cancel, the result would be null, a special value that means "nothing."

As you see, these functions hold everything up till the user has responded. That's OK for testing and troubleshooting, but it's very disruptive for a real situation, so you should limit their use. You'll also find that, by design, you won't be able to change their appearance or the button text.

Modern browsers now support a `<dialog>` element, which allows you to produce much more sophisticated dialog boxes. However, they take more work to set up and process, so we'll stick to the traditional dialog boxes for now.

Arrays and Objects

As you might have guessed, JavaScript also recognizes data that is not simple. These are called **objects** and are essentially more complex containers for more data and functions.

One particular type of object is an **array**. An array is a numbered collection. In JavaScript, creating an array is very simple:

```
»    var fruit = ['apple','banana','cherry','date'];
```

Array items are numbered from zero. In the preceding example, the items are numbered from 0 to 3. You can get the number of items in the array with the .length property:

```
»    console.log(fruit.length);
     4
```

To get one of the array items, you use square brackets for the item number:

```
»  console.log(fruit[2]);
   cherry
```

(Remember, item numbers start at 0.) The item number is usually referred to as the **index**.

You can also change one if the items with an assignment statement:

```
»  fruit[2] = 'cantaloupe';
```

You can also add new items or remove them. Later, we'll work more with arrays.

As we said, arrays are specialized objects. In general, objects are collections of data and functions. However, in JavaScript, you'll find that functions are handled as data, so you can simply say that JavaScript objects are collections of data.

This data can be

- Primitive values, such as numbers and strings

- Functions

- Other objects

In JavaScript, some very important objects will relate to the contents of the web page.

We will look more at objects later.

Undefined or Not Defined?

Although JavaScript may automatically declare variables with or without being asked to, you cannot use a variable unless it has a value.

There are three possibilities:

1. The variable is **defined**.

    This means that the variable has a value. This is usually the result of an assignment statement, though some other JavaScript statements will assign values to variables.

    For example:

    ```
    var x = 3;
    console.log(x);
    ```

2. The variable is **undefined**.

    This can happen if the variable has been declared, but not yet assigned. Such a declaration may be through the var statement:

    ```
    var x;
    console.log(x);
    ```

    This will give the result of undefined.

3. The variable is **not defined**.

    This is not to be confused with undefined, which describes a variable that exists but has no value. If you attempt to use a variable that has not even been declared yet, then it will result in an error. For example:

    ```
    console.log(y);
    ```

    will result in an error.

If you think the terminology is a little confusing, well, you're probably right.

undefined is Not an Error

Unlike other programming languages, undefined is a special value and not an error as such. You can even assign it to a variable deliberately:

»   var a = undefined;

Of course, you *may* end up with an error if you plan to use the variable later when another real value is expected.

Special Value: null

Even if a value has been defined, it may refer to "nothing." This may be because there is not (yet) a valid value. In JavaScript, this special value is called null.

The difference between undefined and null is a source of confusion with JavaScript developers, and even some experts are a little vague on the subject. One thing is clear, and that is even though they both mean a sort of nothing, they're not *exactly* the same.

Generally, however, it's agreed that undefined is when a value has *defaulted* to nothing, while null is when a value is *deliberately* set. This, however, is not a solid rule.

JavaScript Scripts

Every web page starts with the HTML. In turn, the HTML may contain references to images and other media content, as well as CSS and JavaScript.

You'll see later that CSS will also play an important part of our JavaScript projects, but for now, we'll concentrate on how JavaScript is added to a web page.

Loading the JavaScript

There are two main methods to load JavaScript into a page. The first is to put the JavaScript inside a `<script>` element. This is normally inside the `<head>` element:

```
<html>
    <head>
        ...
        <script type="text/javascript">
            //  JavaScript goes here
        </script>
    <head>
    <body>
        ...
    </body>
</html>
```

A script added to the HTML this way is referred to as an **inline** script. A second method is to reference an external file instead:

```
<script type="text/javascript" src="..."></script>
```

As you can see, the `<script>` element doubles up as a link to an external file. In CSS, you would use the `<link>` element to do the same thing, and perhaps if JavaScript were invented more recently, that might also have been the case for JavaScript files. However, that wasn't to be.

What distinguishes a linking `<script>` element is the presence of the `src` attribute. This contains a URL (full or partial) that refers to the external script, in much the same way that the `href` attribute is used to link a CSS style sheet.

Note that if the `src` attribute is present, then any additional JavaScript inside the `<script>` element will be ignored. You can't do both in a single `<script>` element.

Additional script Attributes

The simple `<script>` tag will do the job, but there are some attributes that can be added to affect the script:

- *Very* old versions used a `language` attribute, but that's out of date, so it shouldn't be used anymore. If your browser still requires that, then you can forget about the rest of the book until you update to something a little more current.

- More currently, there is a `type="text/javascript"` attribute to make `<script>` more specific. You don't technically need it either, as the script type defaults to JavaScript, but it can be used to make your intention clear and to help distinguish it from non-JavaScript types.

- The `defer` attribute causes the JavaScript to wait until the rest of the page has finished loading. You'll see more on this in the next section.

- The `crossorigin` attribute affects how scripts from different sources are handled. You'll see more on how this affects error handling later.

The `crossorigin` attribute will probably cause errors if you're not running on a web server. *If you're testing the scripts without a server, you should leave it out.*

There are a few other attributes, but we won't need them for our projects.

In general, our `script` tag should look like this:

```
<script type="text/javascript" src="..."
  crossorigin="anonymous" defer></script>
```

All of our coding projects will include this.

Inline vs. External Scripts

Inline scripts have the advantage of convenience, since you can write everything in a single file.

For the most part, however, it's better to use external scripts:

- Sometimes, you will want the same code in multiple pages, so it's better to keep the code separate and include it later.

- Maintaining mixed code (HTML and JavaScript) is harder and can cause additional errors.

- It's better organized if you use separate files for separate jobs.

- External scripts allow more control over how they are used.

For all of our projects, we'll be using external scripts.

Deferring Loading

In this book, we will be putting the `<script>` element fairly early, inside the `<head>` element, which is standard practice. You can also put the element much further down, and you may even see it placed at the very end of the file.

The browser will normally begin loading and processing the JavaScript as soon as script element is encountered. While it is working on the JavaScript, it will pause loading and processing the rest of the HTML. There are two problems with this:

- Since you *probably* don't want to run the JavaScript till later, you have unnecessarily delayed the HTML content, and users may experience a visual pause in the page.

- Some of the JavaScript will need to reference elements somewhere on the page. Since the JavaScript is processed before the rest of the HTML, those elements won't be there yet, and the whole thing will fall apart.

Modern browsers all support the `defer` attribute:

```
<script type="text/javascript" src="..." defer></script>
```

This will allow the browser to continue processing the rest of the HTML, and the browser won't actually run the JavaScript until *after* the HTML is finished.

Appendix B describes older alternatives to the `defer` attribute. You don't need to do that anymore, but you may encounter those techniques in older code.

You can't use `defer` with an inline script (one without the `src` attribute). If you have inline JavaScript, you will need an older technique.

Error Handling

It's likely that you will make some errors in your JavaScript code, and some of them can be very hard to locate.

Historically, JavaScript was pretty quiet about some errors, reasoning that the visiting user can't do much about the developer's errors anyway. However, as a developer, this coyness can be infuriating, so you'll want the errors to be more obvious.

The following code will make *some* of them easier to identify:

```
window.onerror=function(message, url, line) {
    alert(`Error: ${message}\n${url}: ${line}`);
};
```

Whenever JavaScript encounters a reportable error, we don't want JavaScript to keep it to itself. This simple event listener listens for the `error` event and pops up an alert with the error message, its location (which file), and hopefully the line number.

There are some issues with the line number if the error occurs in an attached file, which is what you'll be doing. The addition of `crossorigin="anonymous"` to the script link should solve that problem.

Note this won't help you with *all* of your errors. For example, some errors will prevent JavaScript from running at all, so you'll never get this or any other message. Some other errors just won't be trapped by this code. However, some help is better than none.

Strict Mode

For your convenience, JavaScript was pretty relaxed about some rules. So relaxed, in fact, that it let you make a lot of errors without treating them as such. Modern JavaScript allows you to be a little more strict about some rules.

To put JavaScript in strict mode, begin your script with

```
'use strict';
```

The `'use strict';` statement is just a JavaScript string. JavaScript will let you put any string or other expression you like as a stand-alone statement, but by itself most such statements are useless, since you haven't said what to do with the values. However, the special `'use strict';` statement will do something as long as it's the first *real* statement in your code or function:

- Strict mode will disallow assigning to undeclared variables. This is excellent for picking up typing errors and the main reason we'll be using it.

- Strict mode has an effect on the behavior of the special `this` variable. We'll see what that is all about later.

This may seem a rather odd way of changing a setting, but it's done this way simply to make it compatible with older browsers. Older browsers can't be expected to understand new commands, but they'll happily ignore a stand-alone string because that's what they've always done.

If you incorporate someone else's code into your own, you may run afoul of strict mode if they have been a little careless, and you're probably justified in feeling a little aggrieved. However, when writing your own code, you should *always* use strict mode.

Note that previously it was mentioned that the `'use strict';` statement should be the first *real* line of code. In this sense, blank lines are, of course, not real code, but neither are comments. In other words, you can have as may blanks and comments as you like at the beginning, but `'use strict';` should be the first statement after all of that.

Some Templates

Putting all of this together, here are some recommended templates for your JavaScript:

HTML Template

In HTML, you will need to include or reference the JavaScript. If the script is to be included inline, you can add

```
<head>
    <script type="text/javascript">

    </script>
    <!--    etc -->
</head>
```

If the script is external, which will be the normal case, you can reference it as

```
<head>
    <script type="text/javascript" src="..." defer
    crossorigin="anonymous">
    </script>
    <!--    etc -->
</head>
```

In this book, we'll be using external scripts.

In some cases, you will load more than one JavaScript file, so there will be multiple links.

If you're not using some sort of web server for the following exercises, the `crossorigin` attribute may cause problems. Instead, you should use the following template:

```
<script type="text/javascript" src="..." defer></script>
```

JavaScript Template

In the JavaScript file, you can start with

```
/*  something.js
    ================================================
    Description ...
    ================================================ */

    'use strict';

    window.onerror=function(message,url,line) {
        alert(`Error: ${message}\n${url}: ${line}`);
    };

    init();
    function init() {

    }
```

This template includes the following parts:

- The comment block at the beginning is to act as a main heading and to allow any additional notes to be included.

- The `'use strict'` statement puts the rest of the script in strict mode.

- The error function will report on some errors.

- The main body of the code is inside a function called `init`, to make it easier to organize. Because the whole script is deferred, it will be called when the time comes with the `init();` statement. Of course, it doesn't specifically need to be called `init()`.

In the projects that follow, we'll be using this pattern.

Summary

- Statements

  A JavaScript program consists of a number of statements.

  Statements are normally written on separate lines and terminated with a single semicolon.

- Expressions

  An expression is a combination of terms that results in a single value.

- Variables and assignment statements

  Variables are named containers of data. When naming variables:

- Use single words only (or camelCase multiple words).

- Start with a letter.

- Don't use special characters.

- Be aware of case sensitivity.

Assignment statements put a new value into a variable:

```
[variable] = [new value]
```

If a variable is used as part of an expression, then its current (old) value will be used.
You cannot put expressions on the left of an equals sign.

- Comments

  Comments are blocks of text that will not be interpreted by JavaScript. They are normally used to

  - Annotate your code

  - Disable (hide) parts of your real code

  There are two ways to write your comments:

  - `// Single Line Comments`

  - `/* Block Style Comments */`

  You cannot nest block comments.

- Functions

  Functions are named blocks of statements that can be reused in your code. JavaScript has many built-in functions, but you can also create your own.

  If the function calculates and returns a value, then the function can be used as part of an expression.

Coming Up

Now that you have an idea of how JavaScript works, we'll put all of that into practice.

In the following chapters, we'll learn more about the language and how to use it. We'll also learn more about using JavaScript to interact with the web page.

First, however, we'll look at some of the JavaScript concepts more seriously. In the next chapter, we'll implement a simple guessing game. In the process, we'll learn more about the main JavaScript structures of conditions, repetitions, and functions. We'll also start working with accessing the elements on the web page.

CHAPTER 2

Project: A Simple Guessing Game

JavaScript can be used to write some pretty sophisticated games, but that's not going to happen here. Instead, we'll write a very simple guessing game. This will help us to develop skills in some of the important concepts in the JavaScript language.

In this chapter, we'll learn about

- Writing a basic JavaScript

- Interacting with the user

- Basic JavaScript structures

- Functions

- Repetition with do ... while blocks

- Conditional coding with if ... then ... else blocks

- Refining the script

The point of this exercise is *not* the game. Rather we'll see some of the important JavaScript principles and structures in action.

Some of the code samples that follow are meant to be tried out in the console. If so, they will be prefixed with the console prompt ».

© Mark Simon 2023
M. Simon, *JavaScript for Web Developers*, https://doi.org/10.1007/978-1-4842-9774-2_2

Preliminary Code

Every web page starts with the HTML. In turn, the HTML will load the JavaScript, and, in most cases, include various HTML elements that will interact with the JavaScript.

In this case, the main element to interact with the JavaScript is a simple button that will be used to start the game:

```
<button id="startgame">Start Game</button>
```

In principle, there could be many buttons on the page, so it is important to identify this particular button. This is done with the id attribute, which is a unique identifier. The actual value can be anything we like, as long as it's unique.

In Chapter 1, we developed some templates for adding JavaScript to a web page. We'll use them here.

The JavaScript code itself can go into a file called game.js, inside the scripts folder, so we can link to it here:

```
<!DOCTYPE html>
<!--    game.html -->
<head>
    ...
    <script type="text/javascript" src="scripts/game.js"
        crossorigin="anonymous" defer></script>
</head>
```

For this project, you would preferably be running some sort of web server, as discussed in the Introduction. If you're loading the files directly in the web browser, you should remove the crossorigin="anonymous" part.

For the JavaScript file, we can begin with the standard template:

```
/*  game.js
    ==================================================
    Guessing Game
    ==================================================  */

'use strict';

window.onerror=function(message,url,line) {
    alert(`Error: ${message}\n${url}: ${line}`);
};

init();
function init() {

}
```

Later in this chapter, we'll move some of the code to a different file. By then, we'll have written a function to generate random numbers, and it's the sort of thing you might want to use in another project.

There will be an empty file in the scripts folder called library.js. We won't need it yet, but it doesn't hurt to have it open.

Starting the Game

The game itself is simple:

- The game will pick a random number from 1 to 100.

- The human (you) will try to guess the number.

- The game reports on whether the guess was too high or too low, or correct.

- If the guess wasn't correct, the human tries again until either the guess is correct or the human gets bored and exits the game.

61

Interaction will be in the form of JavaScript popups, in particular the prompt function that will display a simple message and wait for the user to enter something.

You'll see what the game is going to look like in Figure 2-1.

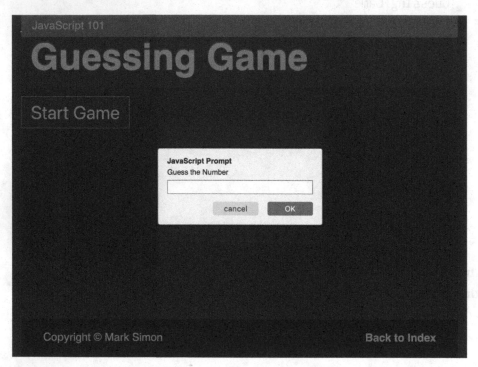

Figure 2-1. *The Guessing Game*

For the game, we will create another function called playGame(). The idea is to trigger this function by clicking on the button.

The first step will be to identify the button and link it to the function:

```
...
init();
function init() {
    let button = document.querySelector('button#startgame');
    button.onclick=playGame;
}

function playGame() {

}
```

JavaScript has had many methods to locate an HTML element, but today the most useful one is the `document.querySelector()` function. This function will take a string which is the same that CSS would use to identify the element. In this case, we are asking for the `button` whose `id` is `startgame`. In CSS, the # character refers to the `id` attribute. This is why it was so important to mark the button properly in the HTML.

As mentioned, the game code will go into the `playGame` function. Here, we have what is called a **stub**, an empty function block that satisfies JavaScript syntax but doesn't yet do anything.

We want to run the game on clicking the button. For that, we will need an **event listener**, which will call a function when the event has occurred. In this case, the event is the `click` event, and the easiest way to assign the event listener is by using the `onclick` property.

The function that will handle the event is, of course, the `playGame` function, so that is assigned to the `onclick` property.

At this point, many newcomers get confused over the use of parentheses. For functions, there are *three* uses of the function name:

- When you **define** a function, it is always with parentheses. Sometimes, these parentheses contain additional variables to be used in the function, but sometimes they're empty.

- When you **call** a function, you are running the code inside the function. Again, you always use parentheses, possibly with values you want to pass on to those variables in the definition. Some functions calculate a result, so the value of the function is the value of the result.

- When you **refer** to the function, you *omit* the parentheses. This means that you plan to call the function later, but not now.

For the `onclick` event handler, you define the function using parentheses. You then assign a reference to the function to be called later; that is, you assign `playGame` *without* parentheses. The function will be called later in response to the `click` event.

Outlining the Script

The game itself will be played within the `playGame()` function. Referring back to the description of the game at the beginning of the chapter, we plan the game as the following steps:

- Set up the game data.

- Repeat.

  The user guesses the number.

  Check the number and tell the user.

- ... until correct.

We'll think of more details as we go along, but that's a good start. We can sketch this in the form of comments:

```
function playGame() {
    // Set up the data

    // Initialise

    // Repeat
        // User guesses

        // Check and report

    // ... until correct
}
```

Using comments is a good way of outlining your plan. When you write the code, they'll also serve as headings.

When you do write your code, you may find that the plan needs adapting, and some of the comments will change or disappear. That's part of the development process.

Initializing the Data

Now to filling in the real code. To begin with, all data in JavaScript is in variables, and we'll need two of them: one for the correct number, which we'll call answer, and one for the user's guess, which we'll call guess:

```
function playGame() {
    // Set up the data
    let answer, guess;
    ...
}
```

We'll use the newer `let` statement instead of the more traditional `var` statement. At this stage, it won't make any difference, but it's a good habit to get into, since `let` is more predictable. Anything done in the console, however, will still use the `var` statement for flexibility.

The variable names may not sound very imaginative, but it's hard to miss their meaning:

- `answer` will be the number the user has to guess.

- `guess` will be the user's guess.

As a *separate* step, we'll initialize the guess to a random number:

```
function playGame() {
    // Set up the data
    let answer, guess;

    // Initialise
    answer = 57;
}
```

Now 57 may not be very random, but at this stage, we need to use a value we already know; you can use any number you like, of course. When developing, you should work with predictable data so that you can see whether the rest of the code is doing its job properly. Once you're convinced that it is, you can work with unknown values. Later, we will introduce a more random number.

Repeating Code

The next part will be repetitive, at least for JavaScript. We want to repeat asking the user for their guess and reporting on the result until the number has been guessed.

JavaScript has a number of different statements to repeat code, but the most generic one is the do ... while statement:

```
do {

} while( ... );
```

You will sometimes see a repeat statement referred to as a loop. It is better to just think of it as a repetition or, later, as iteration.

Here, the block of statements will be repeated while the condition inside parentheses is true.

In the game, we want to repeat the code *until* the guess is *correct*. Some languages actually have an until condition, but not JavaScript. We'll have to translate that to its negative: repeat *while* the guess is *incorrect*:

```
function playGame() {
    ...
    do {

    } while(guess != answer);
}
```

The operator != means "not equal," and JavaScript uses the exclamation mark (!) whenever it needs something to be *not* true. It's supposed to look a little like the mathematical symbol ≠, but you might need to stretch your imagination for that.

This repetition with the test at the end of the block is called a **post test**. It means that the code will run at least once before we decide to do it again.

The Main Play

Inside the repetition, we will get the user's guess, compare it to the correct answer, and report on the result.

Getting User Input

To get something from the user, we use the `prompt` function:

```
do {
    guess = prompt('Guess the number:');
} while(guess != answer);
```

The `prompt` function takes a message to be presented to the user and waits for a response. Its actual appearance will vary from browser to browser, from operating system to operating system, but it will be something like Figure 2-2.

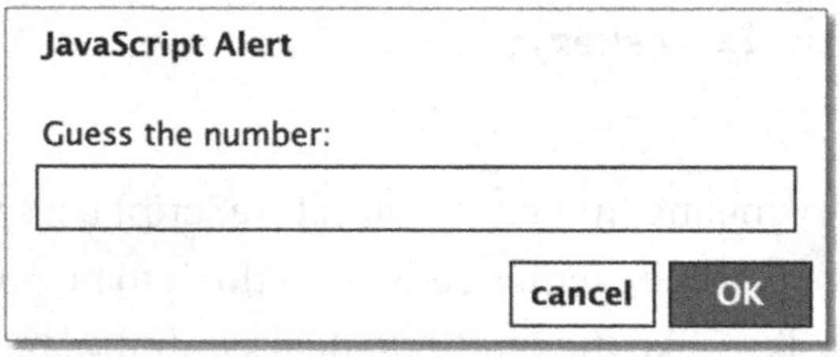

Figure 2-2. *The Guessing Game prompt*

The message here is a little abrupt, but you can supply any message you like.

Note that you have no control over the appearance of the `prompt`, nor the contents of the buttons. This is a small security measure that makes it harder for a website to fake a system message. It also means that you will have to word your message so that "OK" and "cancel" make some sort of sense.

The response from the prompt will be one of three things:

- A string with user input. This comes when the user selects the **OK** button.

- An *empty* string. This is also when the user selects the **OK** button, but with nothing in the input box.

- A null that indicates the **cancel** button has been selected. Any user input will then be ignored.

This response is stored in the variable guess.

Testing the Response

Assuming for now that we have entered something meaningful in the prompt, you will now need to compare it against the correct answer. You can do this using the if statement:

```
do {
    guess = prompt('Guess the number:');

    if(guess < answer) {          //  Too Small
        //  Plan A
    }

} while(guess != answer);
```

The if statement checks a condition inside the parentheses. Typically the condition results in either true or false, but you will see later that JavaScript is a little more flexible with conditions. If the condition is satisfied, the code inside the braces ({ ... }) is run; otherwise, it isn't.

You don't always need braces for the conditional code if there's only one line. For example:

```
»    var a = 4, b = 3;
»    if(a > b) {
         alert('Bigger');
     }
»    if(a > b) alert('Bigger');  // Same Thing
```

In fact, your code will be easier to understand and maintain if you don't clutter it up with unnecessary structures.

In this case, the if clause uses braces because there'll be more code a little later.

Of course, there may be other possibilities for your condition, so you can follow your if with an else if clause:

```
do {
    guess = prompt('Guess the number:');

    if(guess < answer) {        // Too Small
        // Plan A
    }
    else if(guess > answer) {   // Too Big
        // Plan B
    }
} while(guess != answer);
```

The else if clause will only be evaluated if the original if failed; otherwise, its code will be ignored.

You can have as many else if statements as you like, as long as you remember:

- They can't be interrupted with other statements.

- They will be tested in order.

In this case, there's only one other possibility, so we can use the `else` clause statement, which catches the rest:

```
do {
    guess = prompt('Guess the number:');

    if(guess < answer) {          //  Too Small
        //  Plan A
    }
    else if(guess > answer) {    //  Too Big
        //  Plan B
    }
    else {                        //  Correct
        //  Plan Z
    }
} while(guess != answer);
```

This is a fairly full example of the `if` statement. In reality, not all will have `else if` clauses, and not all will have an `else` clause. If they do, however, they must be in the right order.

Reporting the Result

For now, we can simply pop up a message using the `alert` function to let the user know the result of the test:

```
do {
    guess = prompt('Guess the number:');

    if(guess < answer) {          //  Too Small
        alert('Too Low');
    }
```

```
    else if(guess > answer) {    // Too Big
        alert('Too High');
    }
    else {                       // Correct
        alert('Correct');
    }
} while(guess != answer);
```

The `alert` function is similar to `prompt` in that it pops up a message and waits for the user to respond. In this case, there's only one option as you see in Figure 2-3.

Figure 2-3. *The Guessing Game prompt*

For now, each conditional block has only one statement (the `alert()` function), and we would normally remove the braces. However, we'll keep them there for a future improvement.

Testing Your Code

At this point, you can test your code, though you shouldn't be surprised with the correct answer, since it was hard-coded at the beginning. To test it properly, you should try the following values:

- Enter a number that is too low.

- Enter a number that is too high.

- Cancel the `prompt`.

- Enter a zero.

- Enter a negative number.

- Enter a non-numeric string.

- Finally, enter the correct answer (57).

You will notice a few things, some of which will start to become annoying:

- Cancelling doesn't stop the game but is treated as another number.

- Entering a string is treated as a number.

- You have a lot of `OK`-ing to do: one to enter the guess and another to dismiss the message.

When we start randomizing the number, you will see a few other problems.

Consolidating the Message

At the moment, you will get two dialog boxes for each guess: one for the `prompt` and one for the `alert` with the result. It would be much more convenient to combine the result with the `prompt` for the next guess.

To do this, we'll need another variable, `message`. This is because the prompting message will change from guess to guess.

First, add the new variable, and initialize it:

```
function playGame() {
    //  Set up the data
    let answer, guess;
    let message;
```

```
    // Initialise
    answer = 57;
    message = 'Guess the Number';
...
}
```

You can now use the message in the prompt function:

```
guess = prompt(message);
```

That should give exactly the same behavior so you might wonder why we bothered. Even without doing anything else, we have already improved the maintainability of the code by moving the text of the message into the initialization section. This way, all of your arbitrary, flexible values are in one place rather than sprinkled throughout the code.

But the real benefit will be in how we change the message in response to the guess:

```
do {
    guess = prompt(message);

    if(guess < answer) {        // Too Small
        message = 'Too Low';
    }
    else if(guess > answer) {   // Too Big
        message = 'Too High';
    }
    else {                      // Correct
        alert('Correct');
    }
} while(guess != answer);
```

Here, we have replaced the message with Too Low or Too High. It won't show immediately, but since the while statement will go on to repeat, the new message will be displayed in the prompt the next time round.

If, on the other hand, the guess is correct, there won't be a next time round, so the Correct message is displayed immediately using the alert() function as before.

When you test the code now, it won't be quite so tedious.

Randomizing the Number

You're now ready to try this for real. To do this, you will have to replace the hard-coded number with a random number.

JavaScript has a function to generate a random number, as part of the Math package. To use this function, you call Math.random().

The Math package is really a built-in JavaScript object. Its purpose is simply to provide a collection of useful functions and values for mathematical processing.

Like all objects, you reference one of the items using the so-called dot notation. In this case, Math.random() means the random() function in the Math object. For technical reasons, any function that is part of an object is referred to as a **method**. It's really the same thing.

Some other useful methods in the Math object include Math.sqrt() and Math.log10(). Some useful values include Math.PI and Math.E, which are important magic numbers in mathematics.

Technically the Math.random() function gives a **pseudorandom** number, in that it's not really random – the number is generated by a process so complex that we can't guess what it's going to be.

The result of Math.random(), unfortunately, isn't an integer; it's a decimal in the range 0–0.999.... That is, the lowest possible value is 0, while the highest possible value is *before* 1. Mathematically, we would write $0 \leq r < 1$.

What we need to do is to scale this number up to a value from 1 to 100. This will take the following steps:

Step	Operation	Min	Max
Get the random number	`Math.random()`	0	0.999...
Multiply by 100	`Math.random()*100`	0	99.99...
Truncate the result	`Math.floor(Math.random()* 100)`	0	99
Add 1	`Math.floor(Math.random()*100)+1`	1	100

The `Math.floor()` function cuts off the decimal, an operation also known as truncating; this is regardless of how close the decimal part is to the next integer.

If you think the process is a little tedious, you might want to wrap it inside a convenience function:

```
/*  game.js
    ==================================================
    Guessing Game
    ================================================== */

    'use strict';
    function random(max) {
        // returns a random number from 1 ... max
        return Math.floor(Math.random()*max)+1;
    }

    ...
```

You'll notice that we've *nearly* given the function the same name as the original. The difference is that the original is part of the `Math` object while this isn't. Naming functions this way is OK, as long as they are in different contexts but philosophically do the same sort of thing.

JavaScript will allow you to create a function with exactly the same name as another, in which case the new one will replace the old. That's not always a good idea but is sometimes done accidentally.

Functions are an important part of building your code. We've already wrapped our game code in a `playGame()` function, and now we've added another function to support it.

There are many reasons to create functions for your code. Some of the reasons include the following:

- The code can be reused. Here, the `random()` function is a small but useful piece of code you can reuse.

- Once you've written the function code, the rest of the program can just use it without worrying about what's going on inside the function. This lets you concentrate on one task at a time.

- Functions help you to develop larger programs using smaller steps. Effectively functions become building blocks.

For this `random()` function, instead of hard-coding the maximum of 100, we use a parameter variable `max` to make the function more general purpose.

You'll notice that we've placed the new function at the very beginning (after the `'use strict';` statement, of course). That's to remind us that it's there as a supporting function, which might be part of a library. Later, we can even move the function to a common library script to use it in other projects.

We can now use the random number in our game:

```
function playGame() {
    // Set up the data
        let answer, guess;
        let message;

    // Initialise
        // answer = 57;
        answer = random(100);
        message = 'Guess the Number'
    ...
}
```

If you want to test the game now, you'll have to guess intelligently; otherwise, you might be guessing for a while. The simplest way is to guess by halves: start at 50, then half way either up or down, depending on the result. This is called a **binary search**, because you're dividing the possibilities by two.

Technically, the number isn't truly random, but for our purposes, it's unpredictable, and that's close enough.

One feature of random, or nearly random, numbers is that they might be anything. If the number happens to be 1 or 100, well, that can happen, and it's not (yet) a reason to suspect that something's not working properly. Try it again a few times before you start to panic.

Cancelling the Game

For the rest of the improvements, you will be stuck with the prospect of doing a lot of guessing just to see whether your next feature is working properly. You should be able to cancel the game once you're satisfied that your next feature is working.

Remember that the `prompt` function returns a `null` if you click on **cancel**. This will cancel the prompt, but JavaScript has no way of knowing, yet, that you also want to cancel the game. You'll have to tell it:

```
do {
    guess = prompt(message);
    if(guess === null) return;

    ...
} while(guess != answer);
```

Yes, that's three = characters. You'll see why in the next section.

Remember that the whole game is played inside a function. The `return` statement does two jobs:

- Exit the function.

- Set a particular value as the result of the function.

To set a return value, you would use something like `return 'goodbye';`. In this case, we're not setting any particular value, but JavaScript will set a value anyway; the default return value is `undefined`.

For the game, we're not really interested in the return value. We're only interested in the fact that the function is being exited.

Note the `if` condition `if(guess === null)` .... This is a case where a simple one-line `if` statement is more expressive than using a statement block.

Comparing Equal Values

This is a trap for young players. Part of the confusion comes from how loosely we use the word "equals."

JavaScript has *three* operators that use the = character. The first one is the assignment operator:

```
»    var a, b;
»    a = 3; b = 4;                    // assignment
```

The next operator is the **equality** operator and is used to compare two values:

```
»    if(a == b) console.log('yes');  // comparison
     else console.log('no');
←    no
```

The comparison operator uses two = characters: ==. Here, we'll get no, because the values aren't the same.

Now, here's trap number 1. If you use the assignment operator instead of the comparison operator, it will do something, but you won't be comparing the values. Instead, you'll be reassigning a variable:

```
»    if(a = b) console.log('yes');    // assign b to a
     else console.log('no');
←    yes
```

In this case, a becomes 4, and you'll get a yes. But not for the reason you might think. Let's try it again, with different values:

```
»    var a, b;
»    a = 3; b = 0;
»    if(a = b) console.log('yes');
     else console.log('no');
←    no
```

This time, you will get a no. As you see, the only thing that's different is that b is now 0.

When experimenting with the console, you will have noticed that a statement such as a = 3 has a result, which is the value you have just assigned.

In the expression if(a = b) ..., *two* things are happening. First, the variable a gets a new value. Second, the new value is tested in the if(): if the value is truthy, such as a nonzero number, the test passes; if the value is falsy,[1] such as zero, the test fails.

There are many developers around who offer all types of advice for avoiding this trap, but it's all bad advice. Just get used to it. You *will* make this mistake, and you'll eventually get better at identifying it.

As for trap number 2, it is not so bad but can still catch you out. Let's change one of the values to a string and try a proper comparison:

```
»    var a, b;
»    a = 3; b = '3';
»    if(a == b) console.log('yes');
     else console.log('no');
←    yes
```

Is the number 3 the same value as the string '3'? The answer depends on how relaxed you want to be about equality. In JavaScript, one can readily be interpreted as the other, so it's close enough.

If that's not good enough, you can be a little stricter:

```
»    if(a === b) console.log('yes');
     else console.log('no');
←    no
```

---

[1] I did not make up these terms, and they're not real words in English, but they're commonly used. Sorry.

The third operator is the **identity** operator and is written with *three* characters: ===. Basically, it tests whether the values are the same without reinterpreting.

You won't see the identity operator much, but it can be particularly important when comparing the falsy values. There are many values that will be interpreted as false, and occasionally you may need to distinguish between them. That's where the identity operator comes in.

A More Meaningful Return Value

As mentioned, we don't really care what the return value of the function is, since it's just to cancel the game. In a grander scheme, you might actually make use of the return value. Here's how it could be used:

First, set the return value to something meaningful:

```
guess = prompt(message);
if(guess === null) return 'game cancelled';
```

Second, set an alternative return value for the function:

```
function playGame() {
    ...

    return 'game over';
}
```

The way we set up the startgame button makes it a little difficult to take advantage of the return value, but at least we have generated some indicator of why the game has finished.

Displaying the Limits

If you've tested the game a few times, you might find yourself losing track of what you've already guessed. What we can do now is add some feedback in the form of the guessing range.

To start with, the number is anywhere between 1 and 100. If the first guess is too high, then the number will be somewhere between 1 and one less than your guess; if your first guess is too high, then the number will be somewhere between one more than your guess and 100.

You can continue the process by adjusting the minimum and maximum of the guessing range till you squeeze in the correct value. You should be doing that anyway, but now we will get JavaScript to help us to keep track.

First, we'll need two new variables:

```
function playGame() {
    // Set up the data
    let min, max;
    let answer, guess;
    let message;

    // Initialise
    [min,max] = [1,100];  // alternatively: min=1;
    max=100;
    answer = random(max);
    message = 'Guess the Number'
    ...
}
```

The two new variables, `min` and `max`, are first declared as usual and then initialized to 1 and 100, respectively. There are a few notable features of how this is written:

- We have three `let` statements for five variables. You can have as many or as few `let` statements as you like. Here, they are used to group logically related variables in a single statement.

- The new variables, `min` and `max`, are declared before the others and, more importantly, initialized before the others. That's because we will use the initial value of `max` in the next statement.

- Instead of generating a random value up to 100, we use `max`. It's the same value, and we make the point by using the initialized variable. If we decide to use a maximum of 1000 instead, we only need to set it once, which is safer.

- We initialize both the `min` and `max` variables in a single statement.

The expression `[min,max]` = `[1,100]` is called a **destructuring** assignment and allows you to assign multiple values in one go. The square brackets `[ ... ]` define a collection known as an **array**, which we will see in more detail later. The idea is that each variable on the left gets the corresponding value on the right.

Destructuring assignments are not an original feature of JavaScript, so you would have to do the assignments in two separate statements, as you see in the associated comment. It's quite reasonable to put both statements on a single line separated by the semicolon. This is one way of reinforcing the idea that you're assigning two related values.

The next thing is to use the new variables in the prompt message:

```
do {
    guess = prompt(`${message}\nFrom ${min} to ${max}`);
    if(guess === null) return 'game cancelled';
    ...
} while(guess != answer);
```

The message has been embedded in the newer type of string literal, a **template literal**. The most immediate feature is the use of the so-called backtick (` ... `) instead of the usual single or double quotes. This tells JavaScript it can look inside for expressions.

Inside the string is a mix of expressions and ordinary text. Expressions are wrapped inside the special code ${ ... }. In this case, the expressions are just the variables. This is the easiest way of mixing a string with values.

You will also see the \n inside the string. This will work in ordinary strings as well and is a code meaning New Line.

To begin with, you will see something like Figure 2-4.

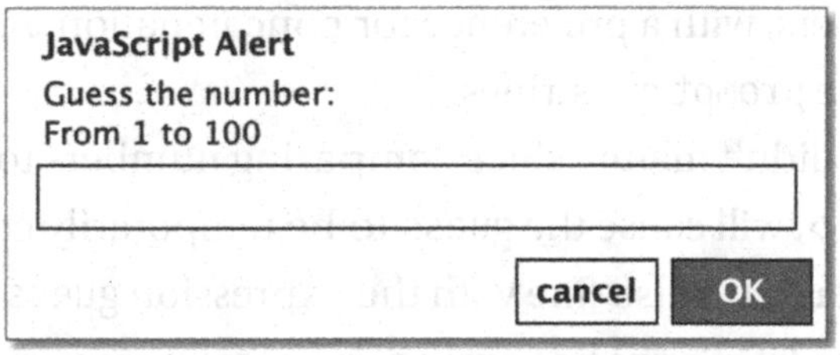

Figure 2-4. Prompt with minimum and maximum

As the game progresses, the limits will change. This can be done while testing the guess:

```
if(guess < answer) {
    message = 'Too Low';
    min = guess + 1;
}
```

```
else if(guess > answer) {
    message = 'Too High';
    max = guess - 1;
}
else {
    alert('Correct');
}
```

That's why we have got the braces for each part of the `if` statement: so that we can include additional statements.

If the guess is too low, you'll need to guess higher next time; the new minimum should be one more than the previous guess. If the guess is too high, your next guess should be lower, and the new maximum should be one less than the previous guess.

When you test this now, it will work a little, but you will see another problem. You may get a message something like `From 501 to 100`.

Here, we run across another problem with JavaScript. Recall the JavaScript uses the + operator for both concatenation of strings and addition of numbers, with a preference for concatenation. As it turns out, *all* inputs from the `prompt` are strings.

Till now, that didn't matter, since comparing numbers to strings, as we do with the < and >, will cause the `guess` to be temporarily converted to numbers for the task. It's also fine with the expression `guess - 1`; you can't subtract strings, so JavaScript has again temporarily converted `guess` for the task.

However, when it comes to `guess + 1` operation, JavaScript will treat them both as strings and concatenate them; this is where something like 501 comes from. The solution will be to force the `guess` value into a number. The simplest way to do that is with the `parseInt()` function, which will transform the `guess` variable to an integer:

```
do {
    guess = prompt(`${message}\nFrom ${min} to ${max}`);
    if(guess === null) return 'game cancelled';
    guess = parseInt(guess);      // convert to a number
    ...
} while(guess != answer);
```

The parseInt() function will generally produce an integer from a string as long as the string starts off numerically, such as 23, 23.5, or 23etc. However, it will fail if the string doesn't start off numerically, such as hello; in that case, you will end up with NaN, Not a Number.

Rather than propagate such an error, we can substitute 0 for in invalid number:

```
do {
    guess = prompt(`${message}\nFrom ${min} to ${max}`);
    if(guess === null) return 'game cancelled';
    guess = parseInt(guess) || 0;      // convert to a number
    ...
} while(guess != answer);
```

The || operator means **or** in JavaScript. It is commonly used to combine multiple conditions, but in this case, it is used as an alternative: if the first value amounts to nothing, use the next value. For this purpose, NaN, together with undefined and null, amounts to nothing.

The Function Library

In developing the code, we added a random() function as a convenient wrapper around JavaScript's built-in Math.random() function. There's nothing about it that's specific to the current project, so we put it at the beginning to remind us that we can use it anywhere.

Now that everything is working, we can finish organizing our code by moving the function to a separate library file.

In the `scripts` folder, there's a file called `library.js`. There's nothing significant in the name – you can use any name that you like as long as you remember what you called it. We'll move the `random()` function to this file.

1. Open the `scripts/library.js` file.

2. Cut the `random()` function from the `game.js` file and paste it to `library.js`.

3. Add another comment block above the `random()` function to describe the function. Something like this will do:

```
/*  random(max)
    =================================================
    Returns a random integer between 1 and max
    ================================================= */
```

4. Add a script link in your `game.html` file:

    `<script type="text/javascript" src="scripts/library.js"`
    `crossorigin="anonymous"></script>`
    `<script type="text/javascript" src="scripts/game.js"`
    `crossorigin="anonymous" defer></script>`

Notice that there's no need to include the `defer` attribute, as loading the file won't interfere with the rest of the page loading.

We can use the `library.js` file in future projects.

The Finished Code

Here is the playGame function in all its glory:

```
function playGame() {
    // Set up the data
        let min, max;
        let answer, guess;
        let message;

    // Initialise
        [min,max] = [1,100];
        answer = random(100);
        message = 'Guess the Number';

    do {
        guess = prompt(`${message}\nFrom ${min} to ${max}`);
        if(guess === null) return 'game cancelled';
        guess = parseInt(guess) || 0;

        if(guess < answer) {      // Too Small
            message = 'Too Low';
            min = guess + 1;
        }
        else if(guess > answer) {   // Too Big
            message = 'Too High';
            max = guess - 1;
        }
        else {                      // Correct
            alert('Correct');
        }
    } while(guess != answer);

    return 'game over';
}
```

Summary

In this chapter, we've explored some important programming concepts using a simple guessing game project.

Comments

Comments can be used to explain parts of the code, as well as to outline sections of the code. They can also be used to disable parts of the code for testing.

Organization

It's best, of course, if you can plan all of your code in advance. However, while building the project, we followed a few organizational principles:

- Declare your variables as early as practicable.

- We used multiple `let` statements with multiple variables to give a sense of grouping of the variables.

- Initialize your data next.

    Sometimes, you can declare and initialize your variables in one step.

- Look for opportunities to write reusable code. If possible, put that code into a library.

    We did that with the `random()` function.

Repetition

The `while` statement is used to repeat a block while a condition is true.

Conditional Blocks

The if statement is used to run code conditionally – when a condition tests as true.

The if can be followed by one or more else if blocks and can be followed by an else block.

Multi-line blocks are enclosed in braces. For single statements, braces aren't required, but they can be used if you think it makes it more readable, or if you think you may need more statements later.

When testing equality, you need to use the equality operator (a == b). It's a common mistake to use the assignment operator instead (a = b), which doesn't test equality but changes the first variable.

Dialog Boxes

The prompt() function can be used to get user input, while the alert() function can be used to send a message.

Cancelling the prompt() dialog box doesn't cancel everything. If you want it to do more, such as exiting the game, you'll have to write the code.

Values coming from a prompt() are strings and never numbers. Although JavaScript will often reinterpret the string as a number if the situation calls for it, it won't if you use the addition operator (+); instead, it will concatenate. Sometimes, you need to convert the string yourself using something like parseInt().

Coming Up

This game was pretty dull as far as a web project goes. The only involvement of the web page was to start the game via a button on the page.

In the next chapter, we're going to have a good look at interacting with the web page. We'll learn how to locate elements on the page and how to change their content or other attributes. We'll even create a few elements to add to the page.

In Chapter 4, we'll put all of that into practice.

CHAPTER 3

Manipulating HTML Elements

All web pages are written initially in HTML, but this code is only text to begin with. The browser then takes this HTML code, together with any associated CSS, and uses it to generate the visible content of the page.

As the browser loads and implements the HTML, it also creates an internal representation of the document for JavaScript. This is called the **Document Object Model**, or **DOM** to its friends. We can use the DOM to manipulate various parts of the web page in JavaScript.

In this chapter, we're going to look at

- Selecting individual and multiple elements on the page

- Accessing and adding content to HTML elements

- Creating additional elements

- Manipulating element properties

- Manipulating the CSS styles of HTML elements

© Mark Simon 2023

M. Simon, *JavaScript for Web Developers*, https://doi.org/10.1007/978-1-4842-9774-2_3

To really get your hands on all of this, there is a sample page for you to experiment on:

- Load the page `sample-dom.html` in your browser.

- Open the Developer Tools Console.

- Also load the page in your coding editor, so you can see the underlying HTML.

To begin with, the page looks something like Figure 3-1.

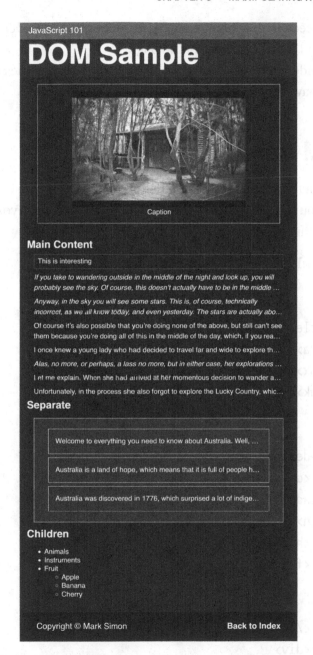

Figure 3-1. *Sample DOM page*

As we proceed in the chapter, you'll be making all sorts of changes to the content and the appearance of the page.

As a reminder that we're experimenting in the console, the code samples will have the console prompt (») at the beginning.

The DOM Tree

HTML documents are hierarchical in nature: elements are inside other elements. If you have a look at the HTML of the sample page, you'll see something of this structure:

```
<!DOCTYPE html>
<html>
    <head>
        <title></title>
        <meta>
        <link>
        <link>
    </head>
    <body>
        <header>
            <div></div>
        </header>
        <main>
            <h1></h1>
            <figure>
                <img>
                <figcaption></figcaption>
            </figure>
            <div>
                <h2></h2>
                <p></p>
```

```
            <h2></h2>
            <div>
                <p></p>
                <p></p>
                <p></p>
            </div>
        </div>
    </main>
    <footer>
        <p></p>
        <p></p>
    </footer>
  </body>
</html>
```

Only, there's more.

When the page is loaded, the DOM is created from the HTML. This is represented as a **tree structure**, with elements branching out to their inner nested elements, such as Figure 3-2.

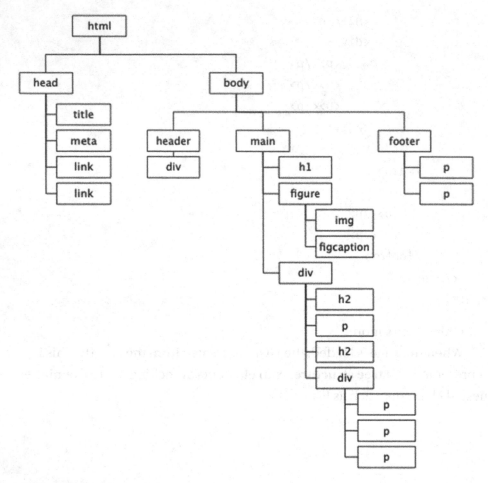

Figure 3-2. *The DOM tree*

The terminology referring to the elements of the tree structure tends to mix metaphors:

- Within the tree structure, the elements are referred to as **nodes**, which are the joints in the branches.

- An element that branches out to other elements is called a **parent** node.

- The elements to which the parent branches out are called **child** nodes.

- Nodes that have the same parent are called **sibling** nodes.

- The starting point of the tree structure is called the **root** node. You'll notice that the whole tree structure is usually pictured upside down, with the root at the top.

Some of the terms come from the tree metaphor, while some come from a family metaphor.

Sometimes, you will need to work with specific nodes, while sometimes, you will work with nodes that are related to specific nodes.

Finding Elements

One thing you will definitely need to do in JavaScript is find the elements you want to work with. In the past, you might have used any of the following functions:

- `document.getElementsByTagName()`: Returns a collection of elements using a specific tag, such as `h1` or `li`.

- `document.getElementsByName()`: Returns a collection of elements with a specific `name="..."` attribute. Today the `name` attribute is limited to form elements.

- `document.getElementById()`: Returns a single element matching the `id="..."` attribute. If there is more than one match, which there shouldn't be, then only the first match is returned.

- `document.getElementsByClassName()`: Returns a collection of elements with a specific class attribute.

These are roughly in historical order. In reality, the last one, `document.getElementsByClassName()`, didn't get much love since it was late coming to Internet Explorer, which was dominant at the time, by which time something better became available.

Note that all but one of the aforementioned functions have the plural `Elements` in their name, to reflect the fact that they return a collection. Only `document.getElementById()` has a singular `Element` in its name to reflect the fact that there should be only one match.

You no longer need any of these functions, but you will still see them in older code or code written by older developers. That's especially the case with `document.getElementById()`. From here on, however, we won't be using them.

There are now two functions that will meet all of your needs:

- `document.querySelector()`: The *first* element matching the selector.

- If there is no match, you will get `null`.

- `document.querySelectorAll()`: Returns a *collection* of elements matching the selector. Even if there's only one, it will still be returned in a collection.

  If there is no match, you will get an empty collection.

You'll get an idea of how they're used in the following table:

Method	Meaning
`document.getElementsByTagName('p')` `document.querySelectorAll('p')`	All paragraphs
`document.getElementsByName('amount')` `document.querySelectorAll('[name="amount"]')`	All elements with name attribute

(continued)

Method	Meaning
document.getElementsByClassName('special') document.querySelectorAll('.special')	All elements in class
document.getElementById('separate') document.querySelector('#separate')	Single element by id

Notice that all of the aforementioned examples start with document., which implies that we search through the whole document. You can, however, begin the search with an element which you've previously located.

For example:

```
»    //  find first div in the document
»         var div = document.querySelector('div');
»    //  find all paragraphs inside the above div
»         var p = div.querySelectorAll('p');
```

Here, the whole document is searched for the first element that matches div. The resulting div element is further searched for all of the p (paragraph) elements.

You'll see more on using the tag names and other selectors in the next section.

CSS Selectors

JavaScript isn't CSS, but it uses CSS selectors in the .querySelector() and .querySelectorAll() methods. A CSS selector is the expression that CSS uses to identify which elements are affected by the CSS rules.

Over the years CSS has become very sophisticated, and there are many subtle ways of targeting elements. For our part, we are mostly interested in the following:

- A **tag** selector references one or more basic elements such as h1 or p.

- An **id** selector references a single element with an id="..." attribute.

- A **class** selector references any number of elements with a class="..." attribute.

- An **attribute** selector references some other attribute of various elements, such as name="".

- It is also possible to reference elements that are **descendants** or **children** of elements, such as items within a particular list or paragraphs inside a div.

Tag Selectors

The basic selector is the **tag** selector. This is a simple HTML tag and refers to *all* elements with that tag. For example:

```
»   document.querySelectorAll('p');    // All paragraphs (<p>)
»   document.querySelector('div');     // First div
»   document.querySelector('h1');      // First (and presumably
                                       // only) main heading h1
»   document.querySelectorAll('h1');   // A collection of
                                       // probably one h1
```

In principle, you would be expected to use querySelectorAll() to get any elements by tag selector. However, there are some cases where the element is expected to be unique, such as h1, so querySelector() might be more suitable.

The older method to get elements by tag name is document.getElementsByTagName(...), but using document.querySelectorAll(...) is more flexible.

Apart from elements that are meant to be unique, you might need further help in limiting the results by using an **id**.

id Selectors

In HTML, there is often an id attached to one of the elements to be targeted. For example, one paragraph on the page has the following HTML:

```
<p id="something">This is interesting</p>
```

In CSS, the id is identified with the hash (#):

```
p#something {
    border: thin solid #666;
    padding: 0.25em 0.5em;
}
```

In JavaScript, you can reference the element using the CSS selector:

»   var p = document.querySelector('p#something');
»   var p = document.querySelector('#something');   // same
»   var p = document.getElementById('something');   // older

Since the id is supposed to be unique, you can use the id by itself, as you see in the second example. However, including the tag makes it clearer, so we'll do it that way.

You will find that many developers still use document. getElementById() as in the last example, but there's no point really. The newer document.querySelector() does the job just as well and is much more flexible.

Class Selectors

If there's more than one element you want to match, then the id is unsuitable. Instead, you'll see the class attribute that describes a group of multiple elements. For example, in the sample document, there are several paragraphs, some of which have a class attribute:

```
<p> ... </p>
<p class="special"> ... </p>
<p class="special"> ... </p>
<p> ... </p>
<p> ... </p>
<p class="special"> ... </p>
<p> ... </p>
```

Of course, the class group may be as small as one, or even none.

You normally think of a group as multiple items, but having a group of only one may make sense. For example, you might want to describe a change in **state**, such as when you click on something.

To match a particular class, CSS uses the dot (.):

```
p.special {
    font-style: italic;
}
```

As with the id, you can use querySelector() to select the first match, but unlike the id, it also makes sense to select multiple matches with querySelectorAll():

```
»    //  First match
»        var p = document.querySelector('p.special');
»    //  All matches
»        var pp = document.querySelectorAll('p.special');
»    //  less specific
```

```
»        var special = document.querySelectorAll('.special');
»    //   older method
»        var special = document.getElementsByClassName('special');
```

There's a subtle difference between p.special and just .special. Many elements can have the same class, but they might not all have the same tag. The second form would also match other elements with the same class.

Child and Descendant Selectors

Sometimes, you want to target all the elements *inside* a specific element. For example:

```
<div id="separate">
    <p> ... </p>
    <p> ... </p>
    <p> ... </p>
</div>
```

To target the paragraphs inside the div, you need a combination of selectors, one for the container and one for the contents. CSS has two methods of targeting the contents of an element:

```
div#separate>p {
    border: thin solid white;
}
div#separate p {
    padding: 1em;
}
```

The greater-than (>) selector is a **child selector**: it selects paragraphs that are *children* of div#separate. The space selector, which doesn't look like a selector at all, is a **descendent selector**: it selects paragraphs that are *descendants* of div#separate.

In JavaScript, you can select a child or descendant paragraph as follows:

»
```
var pp = document.querySelectorAll('div#separate>p');
console.log(pp);              //  children
```
»
```
var pp = document.querySelectorAll('div#separate p');
console.log(pp);              //  descendants
```

In this case, they are the same thing, since there are no other containers in the example. If, however, you start with div#content, you'll see a difference:

»
```
var pp = document.querySelectorAll('div#content>p');
console.log(pp);              //  children
```
»
```
var pp = document.querySelectorAll('div#content p');
console.log(pp);              //  descendants
```

That's because div#separate is inside div#content. The paragraphs in div#separate are descendants, but not children of div#content.

This is also apparent when you have a nested list:

```
<ul id="children">
    <li>Animals</li>
    <li>Instruments</li>
    <li>Fruit
        <ul>
            <li>Apple</li>
            <li>Banana</li>
            <li>Cherry</li>
        </ul>
    </li>
</ul>
```

which looks like this:

- Animals
- Instruments
- Fruit
  - Apple
  - Banana
  - Cherry

You can select the various parts of the list using the following:

```
» var children = document.querySelectorAll('ul#children>li');
» console.log(children);
» var grandchildren =
    document.querySelectorAll('ul#children>li>ul>li');
» console.log(grandchildren);
» var descendants =
    document.querySelectorAll('ul#children li');
» console.log(descendants);
```

In all of these samples, the first part of the selector is ul#main, which selects the main list. From there, we select various children and descendants of the list.

In the first example, the child selector (>) would only select the direct children, those at the first level. The third example with the descendant selector () would select *all* the list items, including the children and grandchildren.

If you specifically wanted to select *only* the grandchildren, you would need multiple child selectors as in the second example.

These are the main selectors we'll be working with, though we'll see some examples of attribute selectors when we start working with forms in Chapters 5 and 6.

Working with Multiple Elements

The result of using querySelectorAll() is a collection of elements, technically called a **Node List**. A Node List is similar to an array in that it is a numbered collection through which you can iterate.

For example, you can get the collection as before:

```
»    var children = document.querySelectorAll('ul#children>li');
```

This gets the collection into the children variable, as before.

There are two main ways to iterate through a numbered collection. First, you can count through use a for() loop to number through the collection.

The for() loop would use a variable to count through the members of the collection and do something with each member:

```
»    var children = document.querySelectorAll('ul#children>li');
»    for(let i=0; i<children.length; i++) {
        children[i].textContent =
            children[i].textContent.toUpperCase();
        // other processing
    }
```

The textContent property is what it sounds like. It's the content of the element as text. You'll see more on textContent later.

The for structure sets up a counter (let i=0) and counts through the collection of children, referencing each member with the index i. The .toUpperCase() method returns an upper case version of the original text.

Note that replacing the textContent will have the side effect of replacing the nested list with only the text: it's no longer another list.

The second method is a newer method that uses the `.forEach()` method. To try this example, you may need to reload the page.

```
»    var children = document.querySelectorAll('ul#children>li');
»    children.forEach(child => {
         child.textContent = child.textContent.toLowerCase();
         // other processing
     });
```

With `.forEach()`, you don't use a counter variable. Instead, the variable `child` is assigned directly from each member of the collection. This is the technique we'll be using later.

The `.forEach()` method contains a function. The example uses what is called an **arrow function expression**, which is a compact form, useful for defining single use functions.

Related Elements

When working with the DOM, you are sometimes interested in elements nearby. You saw previously how different nodes are related. Here is a list of some of the ways you can access them:

Node(s)	Any content	Elements only
Child Nodes	childNodes	children
First Child	firstChild	firstElementChild
Last Child	lastChild	lastElementChild
Adjacent Node	nextSibling	nextElementSibling
	previousSibling	previousElementSibling
Parent Node	parentNode	parentElement

For example (you may want to reload the page first):

```
»    var list = document.querySelector('ul#children');
»    var item = list.firstElementChild;  // get first child
»    console.log(item.textContent);
»    item = item.nextElementSibling;     // next child
»    console.log(item.textContent);
```

The names are clear enough as to what these methods do. The first methods (childNodes and children) return a collection, while the others return a single result.

The first three in the previous table work from the parent node. In this case, it's the ul unordered list, and you would be referring to the li items inside. The last two work from the child nodes. In this case, they're the li list items, and you would be referring to adjacent sibling list items or to the parent ul list.

You'll notice that there are two versions, due to a quirk in the way HTML works. Technically, all the white space between elements in the HTML, and even comments, is part of the DOM. For example, suppose you have a list and items:

```
<ul id="children">
    <li>Child</li>
    <li>Child</li>
    <!-- Nested List -->
</ul>
```

The indentation, line breaks, and comments are all considered DOM nodes. Most of the time, you don't care and are only interested in the list and items, without bothering with the extra spacing or comments. The extra spacing and comments certainly won't appear in the rendered page, so they're only visible if you view the source.

Or maybe if you use JavaScript. Browsers differ in whether they are to be included using the first column properties shown previously, and in the past, that made things awkward. The second column properties only process genuine elements and so solve the problem.

For example:

```
» var ul = document.querySelector('ul#children');
» console.log(ul.children);   // Only List Items
» console.log(ul.childNodes); // May contain other code
```

The second column properties are newer, but all current browsers support them. You probably never want the older first column properties.

Creating and Manipulating Elements

Sometimes, you will need to make changes to the document by manipulating the content of the DOM itself. For example, the first thing you might do is to create an element:

```
» var p = document.createElement('p');
```

The argument is a string that is a simple HTML tag, without the angle brackets. You can even make one up:

```
» var p = document.createElement('thing');
```

but don't expect the browser to know how to display it properly. By default, a made-up element would be displayed as an inline element unless you change that with CSS. This trick was used when trying to convince Legacy Browsers to accept newer HTML5 elements.

At this point, the newly created element has no content and no properties and isn't even in the document yet: it's drifting around in memory. Later, you'll see how to add the new element to the actual document.

Adding Content to an Element

You can add content to an element, whether it's one you have found or one you have just created, using any of a number of methods.

The simplest way to add content is to set its textContent property:

```
» var p = document.createElement('p');
» p.textContent = 'This space for rent ...';
```

There is an alternative property called innerHTML, which, in this case, would give you the same result. However, the difference is that innerHTML will interpret the contents as HTML.

For example, you can change the content of your main heading as follows:

```
» var h1 = document.querySelector('h1');
» h1.textContent = 'Hello<br>Goodbye';
```

In the preceding example, the heading will now say Hello
Goodbye. If, however, you use innerHTML:

```
» var h1 = document.querySelector('h1');
» h1.innerHTML = 'Hello<br>Goodbye';
```

the <br> inside the string will be interpreted as an HTML line break, and you will see two lines of text.

In general, it is safer to use textContent unless you really need the additional HTML.

> There is also a property called innerText, which has had a mixed history. Originally it was an unofficial property supported only by Internet Explorer, while the other browsers only supported the official textContent property. Today, both are supported by all modern browsers. However, there is a small difference between the two, which makes textContent the preferred property.

Adding Other Properties

You can also add attributes as JavaScript properties. For example, you can create an image element using something like this:

```
»    var img = document.createElement('img');
//   create image
»    img.src = 'https://pure-javascript.net/random.jpg';
//   src="..."
»    img.alt = 'Random Image';                        // alt="..."
```

Remember, you won't actually see this image yet. It will need to be added to the document later.

There are two particular properties that you might add, especially for the benefit of CSS:

```
»    img.id = 'something';          // id="..."
»    img.classList.add('whatever'); // class="..."""
»    img.className = 'whatever';    // older alternative
```

Note that for the most part, the JavaScript property name is the same as the HTML attribute, but the `class` attribute doesn't match exactly, since the word `class` is a reserved word in JavaScript.

There are two ways of adding a class to an element:

- The older className property will replace any existing classes with a single class, so it is only useful in very simple cases.

- The newer classList methods manipulate a collection of classes, to which you can add, remove, or even toggle (add or remove depending on whether it's already there).

All of the aforementioned can also be applied to existing elements you have located through `querySelector()` or `querySelectorAll()`.

113

Placing an Element in the Document

This is all a waste of time unless you place the image somewhere on the document. The traditional method involves JavaScript node functions, such as `insertBefore()` and `appendChild()`. There are now functions that simplify and unify the process.

First, you need to find an existing element near which you want to place the new element. You then have four positions relative to the existing element:

- `existingElement.before(newElement)`: Outside, before the existing element

- `existingElement.prepend(newElement)`: Inside, at the existing element

- `existingElement.append(newElement)`: Inside, at the existing element

- `existingElement.after(newElement)`: Outside, after the existing element

Figure 3-3 shows what these functions mean.

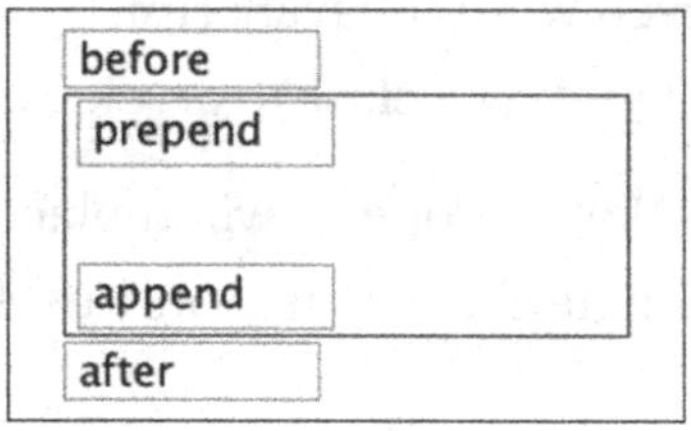

Figure 3-3. *Placing elements*

The functions `before()` and `after()` have a syntax that is unnatural in English. The expression `apple.before(banana)` is read as "with `apple`, put `banana` before it," which is the reverse of what it might appear on first reading. All four of the mentioned functions start with the existing element.

If you look at existing code, you may see the appendChild() function used often. This is nearly the same as the newer append() function. There are some differences, but most of the time, you can use either.

For example, to add a new image after an existing heading, you could write

```
»   var h1 = document.querySelector('h1');
```

```
»   var img = document.createElement('img');
»   img.src = 'https://pure-javascript.net/random.jpg';
»   img.alt = 'Random Image';
```

```
»   h1.after(img);
```

There is also an alternative single function that will do all four of the mentioned functions, given an additional parameter with a position: existingElement.insertAdjacentElement(position,newElement). The position is one of the following:

- 'beforebegin': Outside, before the container

- 'afterbegin': Inside, at the beginning

- 'beforeend': Inside, at the end

- 'afterend': Outside, after the container

Figure 3-4 shows these positions.

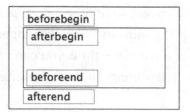

Figure 3-4. *Insert adjacent elements*

Using this function, you can write

»   `var h1 = document.querySelector('h1');`

»   `var img = document.createElement('img');`

»   `img.src = 'https://pure-javascript.net/random.jpg';`

»   `img.alt = 'Random Image';`

»   `h1.insertAdjacentElement('afterend',img);`

That certainly isn't more convenient, but it may appeal to your sense of pattern.

Adding HTML Directly

If you are creating an element only to add it directly to your DOM, you can take a shortcut with `insertAdjacentHTML(position, html)`. This function takes the same position values as `insertAdjacentElement` but allows you to create the element with an HTML string. You can use the same `src` and `alt` values for the following examples:

»   `var h1 = document.querySelector('h1');`
»   `var html = '<img src="..." alt="...">';`
»   `h1.insertAdjacentHTML('afterend',html);`

Of course, you don't need the html variable:

»   `var h1 = document.querySelector('h1');`
»   `h1.insertAdjacentHTML('afterend', '<img src="..."`
    `alt="...">');`

... or even the h1 variable for that matter:

»   `document.querySelector('h1')`
»   `.insertAdjacentHTML('afterend', '<img src="..."`
    `alt="...">');`

but that's starting to become unmanageable.

Note that using `insertAdjacentHTML()` is only useful if you don't need to refer to the new element later in JavaScript, since you haven't got a reference to the new element.

Adding More Complex Content

So far, we've been talking about creating one or two elements. Using `innerHTML` or `insertAdjacentHTML`, you can just as easily insert multiple elements, such as this list full of items:

»   `var h1 = document.querySelector('h1');`
»   `var ul = '<ul><li>one</li><li>zwei</li><li>trois`
    `</li></ul>';`
»   `h1.insertAdjacentHTML('afterend',ul);`

As you know, JavaScript has a new type of string literal, the **template literal**. We've been mainly using it to interpolate values using the ${...} notation. However, the other feature is that this string literal can be written over multiple lines:

»   `var h1 = document.querySelector('h1');`
»   `var ul =`

```
 `<ul>
    <li>one</li>
    <li>zwei</li>
    <li>trois</li>
 </ul>`;
```
»   h1.insertAdjacentHTML('afterend',ul);

Since the string is treated as HTML, the spacing won't make any difference to the result, since additional spacing and line breaks are ignored in HTML. However, it might make the code easier to read, and there are other occasions where the spacing and line breaks are significant.

As before, HTML strings are fine if all you want to do is add the elements, but you won't get a reference to them. If, on the other hand, you need to refer to them later in JavaScript, you will need to create the elements individually:

»   var h1=document.querySelector('h1');

»   var heading = document.createElement('h2');
»   var message = document.createElement('p');

»   h1.insertAdjacentElement('afterend',message);
»   h1.insertAdjacentElement('afterend',heading);

»   heading.textContent = 'Message';
»   message.textContent = `The Time is ${new Date()}`;

In the sample code, it made sense to give the heading and paragraph more meaningful names, as the code will assign them content later in the script. Note that the elements are added in the reverse order, since they insert immediately after the h1 element.

This is the sort of thing we'll be doing in the next project in Chapter 4, on the slide show.

Summary

In this chapter, we've looked at some of the techniques used in manipulating a web page.

The Document Object Model

The browser takes the HTML of a page and renders it into a document. At the same time, it generates an internal model called the Document Object Model.

The DOM is represented as a tree structure, to reflect the hierarchical nature of HTML. JavaScript includes a number of functions to navigate and manipulate the DOM.

The DOM can be modified by adding or removing elements, as well as by changing individual elements.

Finding Elements

There are many functions available to find existing elements in the DOM. Some of these have been available for some time.

Modern browsers all support the newer functions querySelector() and querySelectorAll(), which greatly simplifies locating elements. These functions use CSS selectors to describe the element(s) you're looking for.

Once an element is located, there are functions for referencing other nearby elements in the DOM tree: parents, siblings, and children.

Multiple Elements

Some functions, especially querySelectorAll(), return a collection of elements, even if the collection is empty or has one member only.

To handle a collection, you can use the classical for(... ; ... ; ...) loop, or use the more modern forEach() function to iterate through the elements.

Creating Elements

JavaScript can also create new elements. You can even create elements that have no meaning in HTML, as long as you don't expect the browser to know what to do next.

With a newly created element, you can add content as well as properties, which match HTML attributes. Using the same methods, you can also do this to existing elements located earlier.

New elements need to be added to the DOM using one of a number of functions. These functions place an element near another existing element.

You can also add HTML directly, either to an existing element, using innerHTML, or in creating a new element, using insertAdjacentHTML().

Coming Up

We've looked at using JavaScript to make changes to a web page. In the next chapter, we're going to apply that to creating an image slide show.

In the next project, we'll look at adding additional elements to a page, changing the behavior of existing elements, and interacting with CSS styles. We'll also learn about working with JavaScript Arrays and Objects. Finally, we'll learn about how JavaScript can respond to keyboard and mouse events.

CHAPTER 4

Creating a Slide Show

In this project, we're going to build a simple image slide show. This slide show will cycle through a predefined collection of images at a predefined rate. You'll be able to start and stop it, both with the mouse and with the keyboard.

In the images folder, there's a slides folder, and in the slides folder is a collection of image files, all ready to be presented in the slide show.

The slide show page will look something like Figure 4-1.

© Mark Simon 2023
M. Simon, *JavaScript for Web Developers*, https://doi.org/10.1007/978-1-4842-9774-2_4

Figure 4-1. *The image slide show*

The slide show works by periodically changing the `src` property of the main image.

In this project, we will develop techniques in

- Locating elements

- Arrays

- Splitting strings to create an array

- Preloading images

- Modulus arithmetic

- Changing the properties of an HTML element

- Responding to user events

- Using the timer functions

One thing you will see later is the use of CSS for certain animation effects. CSS is the coding language that defines the *appearance* of HTML elements, and you can use JavaScript to create and apply additional CSS.

If you're familiar with CSS, that's helpful, but it's not necessary; you'll just need a little faith. Just be aware that modern CSS can be used for all sorts of animation tricks which once relied on additional JavaScript. This leaves you free to focus on implementing the logic of your project, letting CSS handle the visual aspects.

The Slide Show Outline

The HTML `img` element defines an image to be displayed. Generally, it takes the following form:

```
<img src="..." alt="...">
```

The `src` attribute is the URL of the actual image. HTML doesn't actually contain the image but tells the browser where to get it from. Normally, the image is local to the website, but it can be a remote image if the URL includes the `http://` or `https://` protocols.

When the browser encounters an `img` tag, it will send off a request for the image referenced in the `src` attribute. Generally getting the image takes some time, so the browser continues processing the rest of the HTML. When an image arrives from the server, the browser will display it in the space reserved for it.

If the image can't be viewed – such as when original is missing, or takes too long to arrive, or when the user is visually impaired and relies on text – then the browser will use the `alt` text instead.

There are three other common attributes:

```
<img src="..." alt="..." title="..." width="..." height="...">
```

The `title` is additional text that may be displayed when the mouse hovers over the image; it's also helpful for search engines to describe the image.

The `width` and `height` attributes are there to help the browser create a suitable space for the image while it is waiting for it to arrive. They can also be used to resize an image.

Our slide show will cycle through a collection of images by changing the value of the `src` attribute, causing the browser to reload a new image.

The whole of the slide show will be contained in the following structure:

```
<div id="slides">
    <img width="640" height="480" src="" title="..." alt="...">
</div>
```

A `div` element is a miscellaneous block container. It's commonly used for layout. Using CSS, the div is made to look like a container for the image.

Preparing the HTML

For the scripting, there should be two JavaScript links:

```
<head>
    <title>Slide Show</title>
    ...
    <script type="text/javascript" src="scripts/library.js"
        crossorigin="anonymous"></script>
    <script type="text/javascript" src="scripts/slideshow.js"
        crossorigin="anonymous" defer></script>
</head>
```

As with the other projects, the slideshow.js file will contain the main code. However, the actual code for running the slide show is something that you might want to use in other projects; you will certainly want it for the slide show variant later in the book. For that reason, this code will be placed in the library.js file for reuse.

Also note that the library doesn't need the defer attribute, as it won't interfere with or rely on the page as it's loading.

For this project, you would preferably be running some sort of web server, as discussed in the Introduction. If you're loading the files directly in the web browser, you should remove the crossorigin="anonymous" part.

The JavaScript Outline

For your convenience, there's already a file called slideshow.js. All it has so far is the heading block comment.

To that, we start with the main JavaScript outline:

```
/*  Slide Show
    ================================================
    ================================================ */

'use strict';
window.onerror = function(message, url, line) {
    alert(`Error: ${message}\n${url}: ${line}`);
};

init();

function init() {

}
```

In the library file, we can add a function to do all of the hard work. This function needs to be given the collection of images and where to put them:

```
/*  doSlides(images, containerSelector)
    ================================================
    Turns a container element into an slide show
    with a collection of images.
    ================================================ */

    function doSlides(images, containerSelector) {

    }
```

The images parameter will be a collection of images, while the containerSelector parameter will be the selector string of the *container* of the image; in this case, the container is the div element.

An Array of Images

When we talk about a collection, we often mean an **array**, which is a numbered collection. An example of an array is

»   `var fruit = ['apple', 'banana', 'cherry', 'date'];`

The number of each item is referred to as its **index**. In JavaScript, the index starts at 0, so the indexes shown previously are 0, 1, 2, and 3.

One thing you will need to know is how many items there are. In JavaScript, this is the length property of the array:

»   `console.log(fruit.length);`
     `4`

Note that since the index starts at 0, the length is *one more* than the last index.

For our project, we will use an array of image names. We'll put that into the init() function in the slideshow.js file. We'll then send the variable to the doSlides() function.

```
function init() {
    let images = [
          'bamboo.jpg', 'bird.jpg', 'bromeliad.jpg',
          'bush-panorama.jpg', 'canal.jpg', 'church.jpg',
          'cityscape.jpg', 'emu.jpg', 'gum-nuts.jpg',
          'hanging-rock.jpg', 'hut.jpg', 'koala.jpg',
          'kookaburra.jpg', 'lake.jpg', 'lantern.jpg',
          'light-house.jpg', 'lorikeet.jpg', 'mountain-panorama.jpg',
          'rocks.jpg', 'rose.jpg', 'steps.jpg',
          'sunset.jpg', 'tall-trees.jpg', 'tea-leaf.jpg',
          'train.jpg','waterfall.jpg'
    ];
}
```

That's a lot of images, and we had to resort to writing the list over multiple lines. In some cases, it might make more sense to write one item per line.

If you don't feel like typing it in, there's a snippet for this array.

Of course, this isn't really a collection of images. It's a collection of file names, and we'll need to turn that into actual images later in the code by adding the images/slides/ folder to the file names and putting that into the src attribute.

You might decide that asking JavaScript to manage such a large collection is risky or inconvenient. Later we will look at how JavaScript can read this list from an external file, using Ajax.

Using this collection, you will invoke the doSlides() function in the library, giving it the images collection and a reference to the container:

```
// slideshow.js
function init() {
    let images = [...];
    doSlides(images, 'div#slides');
}
```

The div#slides string is the same as the CSS selector and means "the div whose id is slides." JavaScript will then use this string in the document.querySelector() function to locate the actual element.

Populating the Image

Currently, the img element is empty, since there's no valid src value. We will change that in our code.

First, you'll need to actually fetch the container element as well as the inner img element:

```
// library.js
function doSlides(images, containerSelector) {
    // Elements
    let container = document.querySelector(containerSelector);
    let img = container.querySelector('img');
}
```

The container variable will reference the containing div element, which will be important for some of the more sophisticated parts of the slide show. The img variable will reference the actual img element, whose src attribute we'll be setting.

Normally, you would locate an element using document.querySelector(), as we did with the container element. This searches the whole document for the first match. However, you can also limit your search to inside a particular element, as we did with the img element: container. querySelector() will only search with the container element. Not only is this slightly faster, as JavaScript doesn't have to look in the wrong place, it will ignore other img elements in which we're not interested.

Populating the image is a matter of setting the src attribute of the img element. We can try it with one particular image:

```
function doSlides(images, containerSelector) {
    // Elements
    let container = document.querySelector(container
    Selector);
    let img = container.querySelector('img');
    img.src = 'images/slides/bamboo.jpg';
}
```

As the images array has only the file names, we've added the path of these images, relative to the root of the website. This makes the code more flexible, since we can easily change the location of the images without changing the collection itself.

If you reload the page, you should see the image.

Since we have a whole collection of images, we should be using one of them from the array:

```
function doSlides(images, containerSelector) {
    // Elements
    let container = document.querySelector(container
    Selector);
    let img = container.querySelector('img');
    img.src = `images/slides/${images[0]}`; // ← backticks
}
```

Notice the different quote marks (` ... `), the so-called backticks. This type of string is referred to as a **template literal**. For normal text, the effect is the same as single or double quotes, but template literals allow you to embed values and calculations inside the ${...} syntax.

Here, we have hard-coded the path but interpolated the actual image file name.

If you reload the page, you should see the same image. At least you'll see that it's working.

Of course, you will want to set the img.src repeatedly for each new image, so it is best to put this inside a function:

```
function doSlides(images, containerSelector) {
    // Elements
        let container = document.querySelector(containerSelector);
        let img = container.querySelector('img');

    next();

    function next() {
        // Populate Image
        img.src = `images/slides/${images[0]}`;
    }
}
```

By putting this in a function, you will be able to call the code repeatedly. You can also defer calling it for a short while:

```
function doSlides(images, containerSelector) {

    ...

    setTimeout(next, 3000);
    // next();

    ...

}
```

130

The setTimeout() function takes a reference to the function to be called (next) and a number of milliseconds to wait (3000). You may also see it written as windows.setTimeout(). Here, you are waiting three seconds before calling the function.

Now if you reload the page, it will take three seconds for the image to appear.

Note that the *reference* to the function is next, without parentheses. If you wanted the *result* of the function, you would use the parentheses (next()). Here, we don't want the result, but the function itself.

Of course, the next() function is still hard-coded to show the first image (index 0). To cycle through the image collection, you need to

- Set a variable for the index

  We'll use the variable slideNumber and sct it in a new Variables section.

- Use the variable

  This replaces the index 0 in the images array.

- Increment the value of the variable

  We can do that with the increment operator: slideNumber++.

- Repeat the call to the function

  The setTimeout() function calls the next function *once*, after a delay. This is how you get those annoying pop-up dialogs a short while after you visit a website. To call the function repeatedly, you will need to replace it with setInterval().

```
function doSlides(images, containerSelector) {
    // Elements
        let container = document.querySelector(container
        Selector);
        let img = container.querySelector('img');

    // Variables
        let slideNumber = 0;

    // setTimeout(next, 3000);
    setInterval(next, 3000);
    // next()

    function next() {
        // Populate Image
            img.src = `images/slides/${images[slideNumber]}`;
            slideNumber++;
    }
}
```

The expression slideNumber++ is more convenient than using slideNumber = slideNumber + 1 and *even more* convenient if you combine it with the previous expression:

```
    function next() {
        // Populate Image
            img.src = `images/slides/${images[slideNumber++]}`;
    }
```

In this expression, the slideNumber++ is called the **post-increment** operator, since the variable is incremented only *after* its value has been used. The **pre-increment** operator ++slideNumber would have incremented the variable before its value is used. There are also the **decrement** operators (--).

If you run this version, it will work, but you will eventually see a new problem. (If "eventually" is too long to wait, you can shorten the delay to, say, 1000 to see the problem sooner.)

The code will keep going past the end of the array. The value of slideNumber will keep incrementing beyond the upper limit of the array, so you will get undefined from there on. You won't actually see undefined, but you will see that the image is now missing.

This will require resetting the slideNumber when you get to the end:

```
function next() {
    //  Populate Image
        img.src = `images/slides/${images[slideNumber++]}`;

    // Wrap Around
        if(slideNumber >= images.length) slideNumber = 0;
}
```

Remember that the length of an array is one *more* than the last index, so when you reach that value (slideNumber == images.length), you have already gone too far. As a matter of policy, you should always check whether you have gone even further (slideNumber >= images.length) in case you missed it before. For example, you already know that repeatedly adding 0.1 doesn't always result in a simple result.

This will do the job, but there are two improvements you can easily make. First, there is a delay before the first image is displayed, and second, the delay between slides should be more configurable.

Showing the First Slide

The setInterval() function waits until the delay is over before it calls the next() function. You can display the first slide immediately by calling the next() function at the beginning:

```
function doSlides(images, containerSelector) {
    ...
    setInterval(next, 3000);
    next();
    ...
}
```

This will now start with the first slide, with subsequent slides cycling through.

Altering the Delay

As a principle, you shouldn't hard-code arbitrary values in the middle of the code. It is better to set the value in a variable early on.

In this case, the actual value of the delay is not fundamental to the logic of the code, so we will set it in a function parameter and let the calling code decide what it is to be.

In the main code, include the delay as an additional argument:

```
// slideshow.js
   function init() {
       let images = [...];
       doSlides(images, 'div#slides', 3000);
   }
```

In JavaScript, it is not an error to include extra function arguments which the function wasn't expecting. This is unlike most other programming languages. What this means is that if you try the code without making any more changes, it will work: the doSlides() function will simply ignore the extra value.

Of course, the extra value isn't there to be ignored, so in the library function, include an additional parameter variable:

```
// library.js
function doSlides(images, containerSelector, delay=3000) {
    ...
}
```

The third parameter includes a default: if the calling function omits a third argument, then this will be the value. This ensures that old behavior is still intact, since originally the third argument wasn't required.

When making improvements to a function, you should always try to maintain behavior compatibility with earlier versions. Here, we've included the default so that without adding the extra argument, it will still work the same way as before.

Obviously, in this case, the slideShow() function is still in development, so there's no compatibility issue to worry about. However, we've gone through the motions to make the point.

Finally, use the variable instead of the hard-coded value in the setInterval() function:

```
function doSlides(images, containerSelector, delay=3000) {
    ...
    setInterval(next, delay);
    next();
    ...
}
```

For testing purposes, you might speed up the slide show by using a short delay value, such as with doSlides(images, 'div#slides', 1000); or even shorter.

Stopping and Starting the Slide Show

You've probably got to the point where the slide show is beginning to annoy you. It will certainly annoy users if you subject them to an unstoppable animation, like the animated gifs of yore. The least you can do is to give users the chance to pause the slide show, which is much better that forcing the user to go to another site.

Although you can write code to pause a slide show when the mouse is over the image, this is not the most natural approach. It is better to supply a button to pause. The same button will also resume the slide show. A button that switches between two states (running and paused) is often referred to as a **toggle**.

Later, we will add a genuine button using JavaScript. For now, we can use the image itself as a button.

To implement a toggle, we will take the following steps:

- Create a variable to hold the current state.

- Create a function to pause or resume the slide show, depending on the state.

- Set the function to respond to a click on the image.

The State Variable

To begin with, we will add a new variable, running:

```
function doSlides(images, containerSelector, delay=3000) {
    // Elements
    ...
    // Variables
    let slideNumber = 0;
    let running;    // undefined
    ...
}
```

All variables in JavaScript begin life with a special value, undefined. This word is confusing, since it doesn't mean that it is *not defined*. The undefined value is a special value used to indicate that you have left it empty. Other programming languages don't have this special value and would generate errors if you attempt to use a variable before it is given a real value.

To set the state variable, assign the result of the setInterval() function:

```
function doSlides(images, containerSelector, delay=3000) {
    ...
    running = setInterval(next, delay);
    next();
    ...
}
```

In JavaScript, all functions return a value. If there isn't a specific return statement, the function will return with a value of undefined. You can either use this value, such as assigning it to a variable, or ignore the return value completely, as we have done before now.

The setInterval() can, in principle, be used on many functions. Each call creates what is referred to as a timer. The return value of setInterval() is the intervalID, a reference to the newly created timer. This is just in case you want to clear the timer, which is how we will pause the slide show.

The setTimeout() function we used earlier works the same way, and you can use the return value to cancel a deferred function call.

The Toggle Function

Since we expect to be stopping and starting the slide show multiple times, it is no longer appropriate to start it once immediately. Instead, we should put the process inside another function and call the function when needed. In this case, we will call it the `toggle()` function:

```
function doSlides(images, containerSelector, delay=3000) {
    ...
    // setInterval moved to inside toggle():
    next();

    function toggle() {
        running = setInterval(next, delay);
        next();
    }

    function next() {
        ...
    }
}
```

There is no technical need to define the `toggle()` function *before* the `next()` function; JavaScript will process all the function definitions before the code is actually run. It doesn't actually matter if you decide to define it *after*.

That's not so true if you're writing code in the console. Because the console has no way of knowing what you're going to type next, you need to define whatever you're going to refer to first.

The role of the `toggle()` function is to start the slide show if it's not already running, or to stop it if it is. That will require an `if ... else`:

```
function toggle() {
    if(!running) {
        running = setInterval(next, delay);
        next();
    }
    else {

    }
}
```

Remember that `if()` will test for a `true` value, but also for a "something" value such as a nonzero number, or a non-empty string. The special `undefined` value definitely counts as "nothing," so `!running` would test if it is `undefined`.

To stop the slide show, you use the `clearInterval()` function, which takes as its parameter the interval id previously saved. You will also have to reset the `running` value for next time.

```
function toggle() {
    if(!running) {
        ...
    }
    else {
        clearInterval(running);
        running = undefined;
    }
}
```

As it turns out, the `clearInterval()` function returns `undefined`. We can take advantage of this by assigning it to the `running` variable:

```
function toggle() {
    if(!running) {
        ...
    }
    else {
        running = clearInterval(running);
    }
}
```

At this stage, if you test the code, you will find that, so far, clicking on the image will do nothing.

Clicking on the Image

For now, we will let clicking on the image pause or resume the slide show, effectively making the image a big button.

A user action such as a mouse click or typing a character is called an **event**. The code that responds to an event is called an **event listener**. The event listener is always a function.

Here, we will assign the toggle function as an event listener on the img element.

There are usually two ways to set an event listener. The classic way is to set one of the event listening properties directly:

```
function doSlides(images, containerSelector, delay=3000) {
    ...
    img.onclick = toggle;
    next();
    ...
}
```

If you try this, the slide show won't have started yet, since it's now waiting for you to click on the image.

140

The onclick event listener property will trigger when you click the mouse on the element, or touch on the element on a touch screen. Again you use toggle function without parentheses, since you are referring to the function, but not (yet) calling it.

Resist the urge to spell the property as onClick. JavaScript will accept the assignment, but since the name is case sensitive, it won't react to the click event.

The same applies to onlick, which is a remarkably common typo.

There are many event listening properties available such as .onmouseover to detect hovering the mouse over the element, or .onkeyup to detect keyboard activity.

Adding an event listener this way is simple, but it has some disadvantages:

- You can only add a single event listener this way.

- If the element is inside another element with an event listener, you have no control over which happens first.

- There are some (newer) event types that do not have simple event listener properties such as onclick.

A newer more comprehensive method is to use the addEventListener() function:

```
function doSlides(images, containerSelector, delay=3000) {
    ...
    img.addEventListener('click', toggle);
    next();
    ...
}
```

In this case, there are no specific disadvantages to using the `.onclick` property, and many JavaScript developers will prefer the `.onclick` method, but here, we will use the newer method in case we need its flexibility later. The `addEventListener()` function can also have additional options to control its behavior.

Here's another typographic point. The actual event type is called `click`, which is what you type in the `addEventListener()` function. The event listener *property* is called `.onclick`. Again, you can't afford to vary the spelling.

At this point, the slide show will load the first image, by virtue of the `next()` function call. It will then wait for the user to click on the image to start it. If you feel that it should start immediately, you can replace the `next()` function call with `toggle()`:

```
function doSlides(images, containerSelector, delay=3000) {
    ...
    img.addEventListener('click', toggle);
    // next();     // wait for user to start
    toggle();      // start now
    ...
}
```

Here, the `next()` function call is commented out rather than deleted. This way, it is easy to choose between the two behaviors.

Prefetching the Image

You're probably testing all of this on your own computer, so you won't experience any delay over the Internet. In real life, the user will first experience an additional pause while the browser fetches the next image. However, that pause disappears after the first round.

The reason for this behavior is as follows:

- First, the image takes a little while to arrive over the Internet.

- To eliminate further waiting, the browser will then save a copy of the image in a local area called the **cache**. The *next* time the same image is needed, it will be fetched from the cache, so you won't get the same pause.

If you want to eliminate waiting for the image the *first* time, the trick is to fetch the image before we need it, so it can be added to the cache for when we need it. This is called **prefetch**.

To prefetch an image, we will first create an image object. This object will not be displayed but simply exist in memory. As we display one image, we will also populate this new object with the next image in the array. The delay in loading the image will be absorbed while the user is looking at the current image.

To create a new image object, we call a special function called Image():

```
function doSlides(images, containerSelector, delay=3000) {
    // Elements

        ...
        let prefetch = new Image();
    ...

}
```

The Image() function is called a **constructor** function and is used to create an **object**. An object is a package of data. There are many built-in constructor functions, such as Date(), which will create an object for processing dates and times. You can also create your own constructor functions to create custom objects.

Constructor functions are called with the special new keyword. In principle, the parentheses would contain additional arguments to help set up the object. If there are no arguments to be supplied, you can call the constructor without parentheses: let prefetch = new Image;.

There are also some functions that create objects that are *not* constructor functions, such as createElement(), which we will see later. They will have their own way of creating an object.

Meanwhile, the prefetch object will simply lie about in memory, as a virtual image. The only thing we want to do with it is to set its src property to force the browser to load another image. This is inside the next() function:

```
function next() {
    // Populate Image
        img.src = `images/slides/${images[slideNumber++]}`;

    // Wrap Around
        if(slideNumber>=images.length) slideNumber = 0;

    // Prefetch
        prefetch.src = `images/slides/${images[slideNumber]}`;
}
```

Here, you first increment the slide number (slideNumber++) and use that new value to populate prefetch. If you're copying and pasting, remember *not* to increment slideNumber again.

Adding a Button to the Document

Clicking on the image is fine for pausing the slide show, but you might feel that there really should be a proper button. At this point, you will have to make a philosophical decision.

A good JavaScript script should be as unobtrusive as possible and require as little help from HTML as possible. HTML has supplied a container for the images but shouldn't be required to supply any more than that, such as additional buttons. You might also consider whether HTML might supply even less.

Instead of defining the button in HTML, we will create one using JavaScript and insert the button somewhere suitable. We will even set its text through JavaScript.

Creating a Button Element

First, create a button element using document.createElement():

```
function doSlides(images, containerSelector, delay=3000) {
    // Elements
    ...
    // Add Button
    let button = document.createElement('button');

    // Variables
    ...
}
```

The document.createElement() function will create a button element, but it's currently in memory only. Shortly we will move it to the actual document. Before we do, we need to supply it with some essential properties:

```
function doSlides(images, containerSelector, delay=3000) {
    ...
    // Add Button
    let button = document.createElement('button');
    button.id = 'run-button';
    button.textContent = 'Start';
    ...
}
```

The textContent property sets what you see on the page. We will change it as we pause or resume the slide show.

The id isn't strictly necessary, as we won't need it to make it work. However, if you want any control over its appearance, you will need to target it in CSS. The attached CSS file has style rules for button#run-button; you can, of course, use any id you like, as long as you modify your CSS accordingly.

The whole point of the button is to pause and resume the slide show, so we will attach the event listener as we did with the image:

```
function doSlides(images, containerSelector, delay=3000) {
    ...

    img.addEventListener('click', toggle);
    button.addEventListener('click', toggle);

    ...
}
```

Finally, we need to add the button element to the document instead. There are many places you can put your button, but it makes sense to put the button somewhere around the div element that contains the img element. This is easily done with the insertAdjacentElement() function.

We had a look at the insertAdjacentElement() function in Chapter 3.

In our case, we will add the button inside the container at the end:

```
function doSlides(images, containerSelector, delay=3000) {
    ...
    let button = document.createElement('button');
    button.id = 'run-button';
    button.textContent = 'Start';
    container.insertAdjacentElement('beforeend', button);
    ...
}
```

If you don't see the new button clearly, move your mouse over a faint image of it at the bottom right corner of the container. The CSS is responsible for placing it over the image, dimming it out, and highlighting it when the mouse is over. The relevant part of the CSS looks a little like this:

```
button#run-button {
    ...
    position: absolute;
    bottom: 1em; right: 1em;
    opacity: .2;
    transition: opacity 500ms;
}
button#run-button:hover {
    opacity: 1;
}
```

At this point, you might decide that you don't need the whole image to act as a button:

```
//  img.addEventListener('click', toggle);
```

The statement is commented out rather than deleted in case you would rather use it after all.

The problem now is that the text of the button is confusing.

Changing the Button Text

Initially the button text says Start. It should change to Stop when the slide show is running and back to Start when it is paused. This should be done in the toggle() function.

```
function toggle() {
    if(!running) {
        running = setInterval(next, delay);
        next();
        button.textContent = 'Stop';
    }
    else {
        running = clearInterval(running);
        button.textContent = 'Start';
    }
}
```

The button will now make more sense.

Changing the Appearance

When the slide show is paused or running, you can change the appearance using CSS. The idea is to use a CSS class.

In CSS, a **class** can be used to describe a variation on an element. You can have several elements with the same class, in which case CSS will apply the same properties to them.

Using JavaScript, you can assign or un-assign a class to an element. The CSS would then apply or unapply the class properties accordingly. In older versions of JavaScript, you would have to use a property called .className. However, this has been superseded by the classList property, which allows you to assign multiple classes and makes it easy to manipulate them.

To add a class to an element, use .classList.add(...) with the name of the class; to remove it, use .classList.remove():

```
function toggle() {
    if(!running) {
        running = setInterval(next, delay);
        next();
        button.textContent = 'Stop';
        container.classList.add('running');
    }
    else {
        running = clearInterval(running);
        button.textContent = 'Start';
        container.classList.remove('running');
    }
}
```

The relevant part of the CSS is

```
div#slides {
    outline: medium solid #666;
}
div#slides.running {
    outline-color: black;
}
```

You will see that CSS will change the color of the border when the slide show is paused or running.

Responding to a Keypress

We have added a button to pause and resume the slide show, but it would be just a little more convenient if we could do that with a keypress. Here, we can use the space bar.

If you have form input or a `textarea` element, you can set up an event listener to respond to particular key strokes within that element. In this case, we want the whole document to respond to the space bar, so we will assign an event listener to the document itself:

```
document.onkeypress = ...;
```

The event listener is for the `keypress` event, and here we can use the simple form. As mentioned before, an event listener is always a function, such as the `toggle` function. In this case, we will need a different function to first test which key was pressed and then call the `toggle` function.

So far, we've created a function by name and assigned the function as an event listener, something like this:

```
button.onclick = toggle;
function toggle() {

}
```

Defining the function this way is useful if you're going to use it again later. However, you can do the same sort of thing without defining the function separately:

```
button.onclick = function() {

}
```

This is called a **function expression**. Note that this function doesn't have a name, in which case it is referred to as an anonymous function. You might also give it a name:

```
button.onclick = function toggle() {

}
```

However, the name would only be available within the function itself, so you won't see this pattern very much.

For the keypress, we'll use the same idea to create our event listener without creating a separate function:

```
function doSlides(images, containerSelector, delay=3000) {
    ...

    document.onkeypress = function(event) {

    };

    function toggle() {
        ...
    }
    ...
}
```

Note that the function also has a parameter. All event listeners are given a special event object as a parameter, but in many cases, you won't bother with it. You can call it anything you like, but you will commonly see it named as event, e, or even evt.

JavaScript allows you to ignore incoming parameter values, as we have done so far. This time, however, we will need it.

The event object contains all sorts of information about the event, such as where the mouse was when it happened, whether the shift key was also pressed, and which key triggered the event. The key that was pressed is in the .key property, and we can test it with a simple if():

```
document.onkeypress = function(event) {
    if(event.key == ' ') {

    }
};
```

Here, we're only interested in the space bar, so we just use a string with a space (' ').

At this point, if the test passes, we can call the toggle:

```
document.onkeypress = function(event) {
    if(event.key==' ') {
        toggle();
    }
};
```

However, the browser typically has its own idea of how to respond to certain keys, and that might interfere with our own plans. We can hijack the behavior entirely by telling the browser not to continue responding with the event.preventDefault() function:

```
document.onkeypress = function(event) {
    if(event.key==' ') {
        toggle();
        event.preventDefault();
    }
};
```

Modern JavaScript has an alternative method of writing a function expression:

```
document.onkeypress = event => {
    if(event.key==' ') {
        toggle();
        event.preventDefault();
    }
};
```

This is called an **arrow function** expression, for obvious reasons. Arrow functions have a simple syntax, which makes them convenient for writing event handlers. They also lack some features of their traditional counterpart, which can actually be an advantage in more complex code.

In this case, there is no real benefit to using the arrow syntax, but you will find increasingly that event listeners are written this way.

Adding Caption Text

We can now add a descriptive caption for each image. The captions will be included with the array of image names and displayed in a special paragraph element created within the JavaScript.

JavaScript Objects

So far, the images array contains items with image names only. If we want to include captions, each item will need to be a little more complex.

An **object** is a package of data. JavaScript has many predefined objects, but you can make your own object by defining a collection of object properties:

```
»   var apple = {
        shape: 'round',
        colour: 'red'
    };
```

This is called an **object literal**, as you are defining the properties in the code itself. In JavaScript, an object literal is contained inside braces ({ ... }), which looks just like a block of code but isn't. In fact, the fact that braces are used for two different things can lead JavaScript to misinterpret some code.

Each property of the object can be read as object.property:

```
»   console.log(apple.colour);
```

You can also change the value of the property:

```
»   apple.colour = 'green';
```

Be careful when writing an object property. By default, JavaScript will allow you to create new properties on the fly, which is not always your intention. For example:

```
apple.Colour = 'green';
```

would have created a new property called Colour, since property names, like the rest of JavaScript, are case sensitive.

You can, of course, write an object literal on a single line:

```
»   var banana = { shape: 'long', colour: 'yellow' };
```

If you're going to make many objects with the same properties but different values, you might create a constructor function to do it for you:

```
»   function Fruit(shape, colour) {
        this.shape = shape;
        this.colour = colour;
    }
```

```
»   var cherry = new Fruit('small', 'black');
```

154

We won't go further into creating constructor functions at this point.

Revisiting the Images Collection

Instead of having an array of strings, we can have an array of objects, which will each have the name of the image and its caption. Each object can take the following form:

```
{
    src: '...',
    caption: '...'
}
```

where the src property is the name of the image and the caption is what it says.

We can call this new array images2, to distinguish it from the original collection.

By writing each object on one line, the images array would now be

```
let images2 = [
    { src: '...', caption: '...' },
    { src: '...', caption: '...' },
    { src: '...', caption: '...' }
];
```

You can now define the images array in the sample project as

```
let images = [ ... ];

let images2 = [
      { src: 'bamboo.jpg',
        caption: 'Bamboo Forest In Japan' },
      { src: 'bird.jpg', caption: 'Bird in Flight' },
      { src: 'bromeliad.jpg', caption: 'Bromeliad Flower' },
      { src: 'bush-panorama.jpg',
```

```
      caption: 'Panorama of Australian Bush' },
    { src: 'canal.jpg', caption: 'A Canal in Holland' },
    { src: 'church.jpg',
      caption: 'Old Church in Brisbane at Night' },
    { src: 'cityscape.jpg', caption: 'A City in Japan' },
    { src: 'emu.jpg', caption: 'Australian Emu' },
    { src: 'gum-nuts.jpg', caption: 'Some Gum Nuts' },
    { src: 'hanging-rock.jpg',
      caption: 'Rock Out Crops in Victoria' },
    { src: 'hut.jpg', caption: 'Old Bush Hut' },
    { src: 'koala.jpg',
      caption: 'A Koala doing what Koalas normally do ...' },
    { src: 'kookaburra.jpg',
      caption: 'A Kookaburra Looking Back' },
    { src: 'lake.jpg', caption: 'A Lake in Japan' },
    { src: 'lantern.jpg',
      caption: 'Lantern at a Japanese Shrine' },
    { src: 'light-house.jpg', caption: 'A Light House' },
    { src: 'lorikeet.jpg',
      caption: 'Australian Lorikeet' },
    { src: 'mountain-panorama.jpg',
      caption: 'Mountain Panorama in Japan' },
    { src: 'rocks.jpg', caption: 'Rock Outcrop in Lake' },
    { src: 'rose.jpg', caption: 'A Yellow Rose' },
    { src: 'steps.jpg',
      caption: 'Stone Steps in a Garden' },
    { src: 'sunset.jpg', caption: 'Sunset in the Clouds' },
    { src: 'tall-trees.jpg',
      caption: 'Trees in Australian Bush' },
    { src: 'tea-leaf.jpg',
      caption: 'A Leaf of the Camellia Sinensis Plant' },
```

```
   { src: 'train.jpg',
     caption: 'Train approaching the Station' },
   { src: 'waterfall.jpg',
     caption: 'Waterfall in the Wood' }
 ];
```

To save you too much typing, there's also a snippet for this array.

In the slideshow.js file, you can change the function call to use the images2 array:

doSlides(images2, 'div#slides', 3000);

Of course, you have now broken the code.

Using the Object Properties

Instead of each item being just the name of the image, it is now an object containing the name and the caption. To read the name, you use images[...].src. This will be inside the evaluated expression ${images[...].src}:

```
function next() {
    // Populate Image
    //  img.src = `images/slides/${images[slideNumber++]}`;
    img.src = `images/slides/${images[slideNumber++].src}`;

    // Wrap Around
    if(slideNumber>=images.length) slideNumber = 0;

    // Prefetch
    //  prefetch.src = `images/slides/${images[slideNumber]}`;
    prefetch.src = `images/slides/${images[slideNumber].src}`;
}
```

At least the slide show is working again.

Adding the Caption

The next step is to create a paragraph element to contain the caption and to populate it when the time comes.

To create the paragraph element, we'll use the same technique as for the button:

```
function doSlides(images, containerSelector, delay=3000) {
    // Elements
    ...

    // Add Caption
    let caption = document.createElement('p');
    container.insertAdjacentElement('beforeend', caption);

    // Variables
    ...
}
```

Here, the paragraph is added at the end of the container, after the previously added button. The CSS is responsible for locating the new paragraph in the container and defining its appearance, such as centering and bold-facing the text.

All that remains is for the next() function to populate the caption:

```
function next() {
    // Populate Image
    img.src = `images/slides/${images[slideNumber].src}`;
    caption.textContent = images[slideNumber++].caption;
    ...
}
```

Note that the expression slideNumber++ has been moved to the caption statement. This is because you don't want to increment slideNumber before you've finished with the old value. If you prefer, the following might be clearer:

```
function next() {
    //  Populate Image
        img.src = `images/slides/${images[slideNumber].src}`;
        caption.textContent = images[slideNumber].caption;
        slideNumber++;

    ...
}
```

At the same time, you can also set the title property of the image itself, as well as the alt property, which you can set to the same:

```
function next() {
    //  Populate Image
        img.src = `images/slides/${images[slideNumber].src}`;
        caption.textContent = images[slideNumber].caption;
        img.title = images[slideNumber].caption;
        img.alt = images[slideNumber].caption;
        slideNumber++;

    ...
}
```

The title property of an image is usually not displayed but will show as a tool tip if you hover the mouse over it.

Summary

In this chapter, we looked at techniques for manipulating the contents of a web page, using an image slide show. In the process, we developed a number of skills.

Organizing Code

We put the actual slide show code in the `library.js` file so that it can be reused. The function also accepts a collection of images and the CSS selector of the slide show container to make it as flexible as possible.

Locating Elements

We used the `.querySelector()` function to locate the slide container as well as the `img` element inside it.

Arrays

An array is a numbered collection of items. You can create an array from an array literal:

```
var fruit = ['apple', 'banana', 'cherry'];
```

Arrays are numbered from 0. You can get the number of items using the `.length` property. You can get an individual item from an array using an index in square brackets: `fruit[1]`.

Manipulating Image Elements

In HTML, an image appears in an `img` element. In JavaScript, we manipulated the element by changing its `.src`, `.alt`, and `.title` properties.

The browser will immediately attempt to reload the image once the `.src` property has been changed.

Delaying and Repeating Functions

JavaScript has the `setTimeout()` function to delay calling a function for a while. There is also the `setInterval()` function to call the function repeatedly.

In both cases, a variable can be set from the return of these functions, to allow us to cancel them.

Starting and Stopping

Using the variable from the `setTimeout()` function, we can track whether the slide show is currently running and use it to make adjustments to the appearance of the content.

We can also use this variable to manage a toggle button. The button is used to start the slide show by running `setTimeout()`, or to cancel it if it is already running.

Event Handlers and Creating Elements

Any HTML element can act as a button by setting an event listener to respond to a click. We did this first with the image element.

We can also create an additional button element using `document. createElement()`. By adding an `.id` property, we can allow CSS to style it. The button was then assigned a click event handler.

It is also possible to assign a keyboard event listener to the document itself. We did this to listen for the space bar to toggle the slide show.

Prefetching the Image

Images fetched over the Internet can take a little while to arrive, and this could cause a pause in the slide show.

We created a virtual image to contain the next image in the array. This allows the browser to fetch the image and to cache it while the visitor is looking at the previous image.

Objects

We proceeded to including a caption for each image. This required modifying the array from an array of strings to an array of objects.

An object is a collection of values. The objects used for the images included a `.src` property and a `.caption` property.

We then refactored the code to use the `.src` property of each object.

We also created a new paragraph element for the caption and populated it with the `caption` property of each object.

Coming Up

The next project will involve interacting with a web form. That will be in Chapter 6, on creating a specialized calculator.

Before that, however, we'll learn more about how forms work and how we work with them.

CHAPTER 5

Working with Forms

HTML forms are an important part of interacting with the user. Typically, the user enters data into the form, and it is then sent to the web server for further processing.

JavaScript can also process form data within the browser. Sometimes, this is to allow it to preprocess or check the data before it is sent to the server, but sometimes it all stays within the browser and doesn't need to be sent off.

Traditionally, JavaScript has been used for data **validation**: checking whether the form has been filled in properly before it is sent off. To do the job properly, the web server should check it again: there are some things that can't be checked at the browser end, and it's always possible to bypass JavaScript validation.

To this extent, JavaScript validation is not final validation, but rather for user convenience, since it can warn the user of errors before the form is sent off.

In modern HTML, much of the form validation can be handled with additional HTML attributes, so JavaScript validation is not so important. However, JavaScript still has an important role in working with form data.

In the next project, we'll use a form as a specialized calculator, where the JavaScript will be used to check the inputs and to calculate a result. For now, we'll have a look at how JavaScript can work with forms in general.

© Mark Simon 2023
M. Simon, *JavaScript for Web Developers*, https://doi.org/10.1007/978-1-4842-9774-2_5

How HTML Forms Are Structured

A form is an HTML container and can contain the following types of elements:

- Form fields, such as text boxes, menus, and buttons. These contain the actual *data* of the form, and they're the main point of the form.

- Organizing elements such as `fieldset` and `label`. These have no effect on the data but help the user visually and practically.

- Any other elements, such as paragraphs and images. Again, they have no effect on the data but are used to enhance the appearance of the form or to make parts of the form clearer.

- Of course, these other elements are not part of the form *per se*: they're just *inside* the form. They may just as well have been placed outside the form.

Open up the page `sample-form.html` in your browser and coding editor. Here is an extract showing the structure of the form:

```
<form id="contact" method="post"
    action="https://pure-javascript.net/testform.
    php?page=sample&testing">
    <p>Enter your details:</p>
    <fieldset>
        <p><label>Full Name:<br>
            <input type="text" name="name"
                value="Fred Nurke"></label></p>
        <p><label>Email Address:<br>
            <input type="email" name="email-address"
```

```
            value="fred@example.com">
        </label></p>
      <p><label>Subject:<br>
          <input type="text" name="subject"
            value="General Enquiry">
          </label></p>
      <p><label>Message:<br>
          <textarea name="message">This space ...</textarea>
          </label></p>
    </fieldset>
    <p><button type="submit" name="send">Send Message
    </button></p>
</form>
```

In a browser, the form might look something like Figure 5-1.

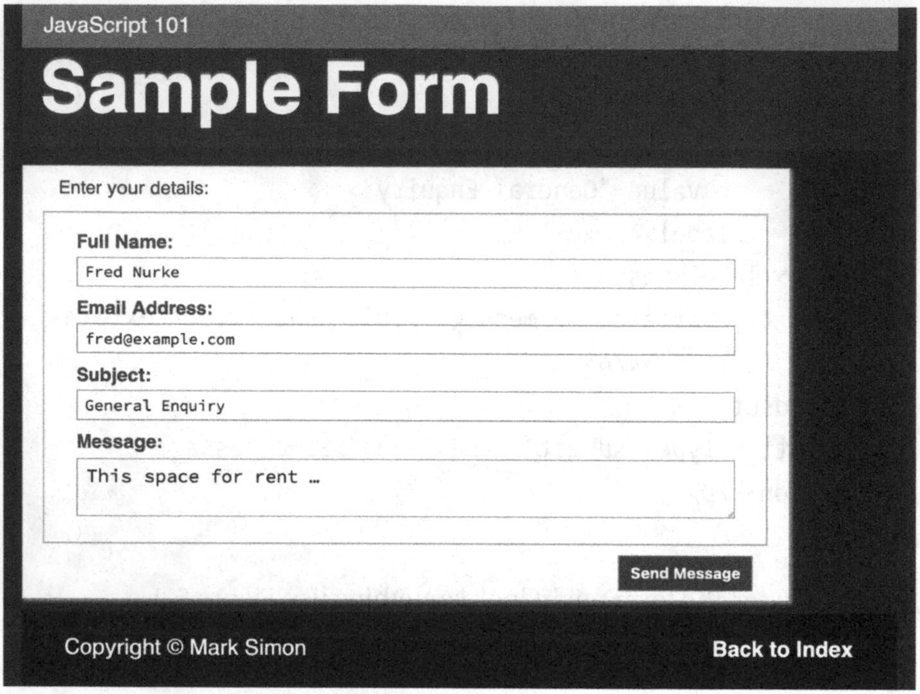

Figure 5-1. The Sample Form

The actual appearance will depend partly on the browser and very much on CSS styles. Modern developers put a lot of effort into making forms look good and easy to use. The appearance has no effect whatever on what the web server sees when the data has been submitted; however, it will certainly affect how the user interacts with the form.

The important parts of the sample form are as follows:

- The form has an `id` attribute. That has no effect on the data but is used by CSS to style it. It is also used in JavaScript to target the specific form.

- The form also has the `method` and `action` attributes that control how data is sent back to the web server. They are important for submitting data back to the server.

- There are some data elements. In this example, they are text boxes of various types, but they could also include check boxes, radio buttons, lists, and menus. We will be very interested in these data elements in JavaScript.

- There is a submit button that is also regarded as a data element. Normally, this would submit the data to the server but can be intercepted in JavaScript.

- Everything else in the form is organizational and won't affect our processing of the data.

Apart from other HTML attributes, form field *elements* have a few relevant attributes:

- The name="..." attribute attaches an identifier to the data. If you are sending the form to the server, the name is the *only* way to identify the values. In JavaScript, there are alternative ways, but we will use the name attribute.

- The value="..." is a *default* value, but the current value can easily be changed by the user. It is normally used as a convenience for the user and will be convenient for us in testing.

  The value is one of the few properties that have *two* different meanings. As an HTML attribute, it is the *default* value; as a JavaScript property, it is the *current* value.

- The type attribute is important for the *behavior* of the form and its elements but has no effect on the actual data.

In this case, the smaller text boxes have either type="text" or type="email", which looks like a text box but is restricted to text that resembles an email address. The larger text box is a textarea element that does a similar job but doesn't have a type attribute.

By default, a button element inside a form acts as a submit button. It's normally better to specify this with the attribute type="submit". The form typically has an action="..." attribute that has the URL where the data will be submitted.

If you submit the sample form, either with the default values or with your own values, the data will be sent off to a script on a web server. In this case, the script simply displays the data that was sent to the server, without processing it any further. You'll see something like Figure 5-2.

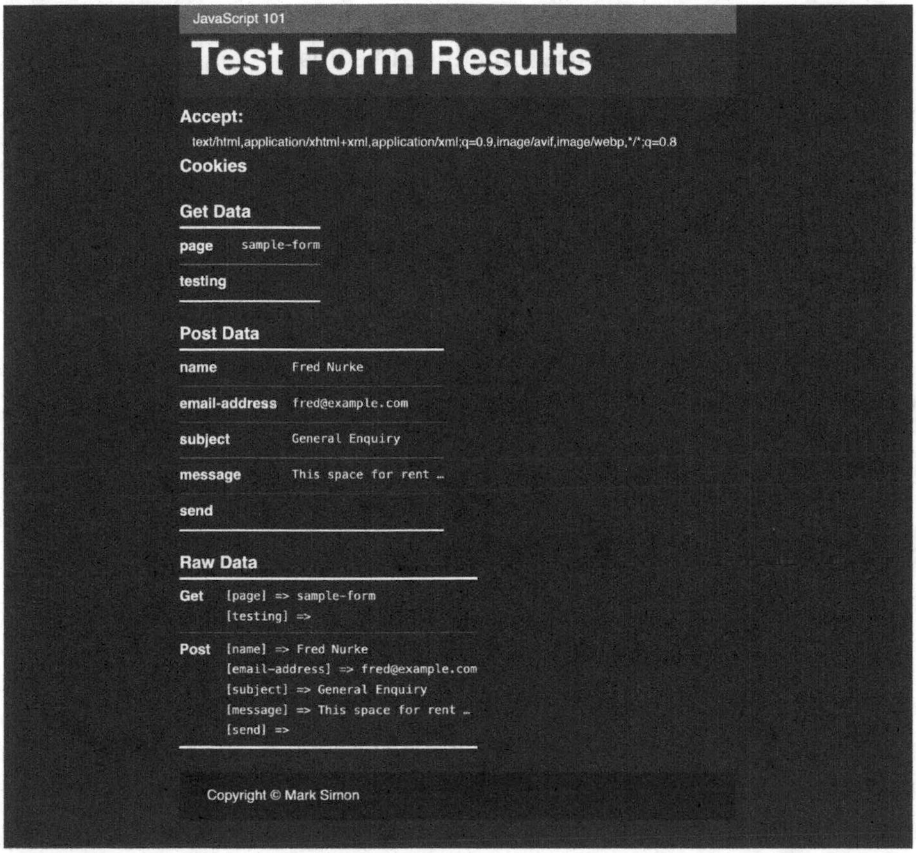

Figure 5-2. *Sample form results*

The **Get** data is the data that was added to the URL in the form of a query string. The **Post** data is the data from the form itself, in which the method was set to post. If the method was set to get, it would have been added to the query string as more **Get** data.

Accessing the Form in JavaScript

For our purposes, we don't necessarily want to submit the form to the server. We just want to access it with JavaScript.

The first thing you will need is a reference to the form. Assuming that the form has an id, you can use something like this:

```
var form = document.querySelector('form#contact');
```

The variable name, of course, doesn't have to be form.

The form's id attribute has no meaning if the form is submitted, and the server will never see the id. However, it is important within the browser for styling in CSS and, as we see here, for JavaScript.

There is also a forms collection, and you could have referred to forms[0] as the first (and only) form, but that's not necessary in modern JavaScript.

Accessing Form Elements

From JavaScript's perspective, a form is an **object**: a complex package. It has many properties, such as the action and the method that are part of how the form itself behaves. It also has a collection of form elements.

There are two ways of accessing a form's elements. The simplest approach would be to use the element's name as a property. For example, to access the element whose name is subject, you can fill in the text box and then use form.subject in JavaScript:

```
var form = document.querySelector('form#contact');
console.log(form.subject);
```

This is a very common approach because it's simple. However, it mixes the form elements with other properties of the form (such as its method or action), and it becomes a problem if you need to access other form properties that coincidentally have the same name as form elements. It is better to access the elements through the form.elements collection:

```
var form = document.querySelector('form#contact');
console.log(form.elements.subject);
```

Another complication is that the element's name attribute may not be a suitable JavaScript property name.

For example, if the name is something like name="email-address", you can't refer to form.elements.email-address, since you can't use hyphens in property names. Instead, you would need to use the alternative notation form.elements['email-address'].

There are now a few ways to refer to a form element:

»   `var form = document.querySelector('form#contact');`
»   `console.log(form.subject);`
»   `console.log(form.elements.subject);`
»   `console.log(form.elements['subject']);   // preferred`

The last way is the one we'll prefer as it's the safest and works for all valid names.

If you run the code shown previously, you will see the element itself, but not the text in the element. For that, you will need to read some of the element's properties.

Accessing the Form Data

All form elements can be accessed using form.elements['element-name']. However, this will give you the element itself and not yet the data inside the element.

Confusingly, there are two relevant properties whose names overlap:

- The HTML value="..." attribute is really the *default* value; in JavaScript, it is referred to as the .defaultValue property.

- The *current* value of the element is what JavaScript refers to as the .value property.

For example, suppose you enter something like Random Question in the Subject of the form. You can then examine it as follows:

» `var form = document.querySelector('form#contact');`
» `console.log(form.elements['subject'].defaultValue);`
  `General Enquiry`
» `console.log(form.elements['subject'].value);`
  `Random Question`

For most applications, you'll want the `.value` property.

If you want to, you can set the `value` property:

» `var form = document.querySelector('form#contact');`
» `form.elements['email-address'].value = 'someone@ example.com';`

You can also set the `.defaultValue` property this way, but it's not very useful.

Note that the `.value` property is *always* a string. If you are expecting a number, you may have to run it through `parseInt()` or `parseFloat()` to convert it to a number. This is the same problem you will have encountered with the `prompt` function in the Guessing Game.

Accessing the Submit Button

The form's submit button is a form element like the rest, so it can easily be accessed using the same notation:

`form.elements['send'];`

- One thing you might do is to emulate clicking on the submit button:

```
»    var form = document.querySelector('form#contact');
»    form.elements['send'].click();
```

- The click() function emulates the click and can be used any time you want to click on any element.

  If you really wanted to submit the form, you could also do it from the form object, using the submit() function:

```
»    var form = document.querySelector('form#contact');
»    form.submit();
```

- The mostly likely use for accessing the submit button is to attach an event listener function:

```
»    var form = document.querySelector('form#contact');
»    function doSomething(event) {

     }
»    form.elements['send'].onclick = doSomething;
```

Note that, since we're experimenting in the console, we need to define the doSomething() function *before* we refer to it. In a real script, you can define the function afterward, since the JavaScript interpreter will scan for all of the function definitions before running the script.

Also note that if you redefine the function, as you will a few times here, you will also need to reassign the onclick event listener.

The attached function is called an event listener and actually has a parameter, if you need it. The parameter, often called event, can be used to cancel the submit:

```
»   var form = document.querySelector('form#contact');
»   function doSomething(event) {
        //  process form
        event.preventDefault();
    }
»   form.elements['send'].onclick = doSomething;
```

Since the default behavior of a submit button is to submit the data, the preventDefault() function would stop this. Sometimes, this is used after an if(), such as when checking for errors. It can also be used unconditionally if you want to process the form entirely in JavaScript without sending it to the server.

You will often see the preventDefault() function called first:

```
function doSomething(event) {
    event.preventDefault();
    //  process form
}
```

If you don't cancel the submit, then the form will be submitted, and in this case, the page will be reloaded.

Summary

In this chapter, we had a quick look at HTML forms. We looked at

- How HTML forms are structured
- Accessing the form in JavaScript
- Accessing form elements

- Accessing the form data

- Accessing the submit button and intercepting the submit process

Coming Up

Now that we know about forms and JavaScript, we're going to use a form as a customized calculator.

In the calculator project, we'll learn more about working with forms and form fields and processing data from the form.

We'll also learn more about techniques in processing and calculating with data and a little bit about storing data for the future.

CHAPTER 6

Creating a Custom Calculator Form

Web forms are a standard method of allowing the user to communicate back to the web server. This is often to send messages or to place orders. Although forms will work as they are, they are often supplemented with JavaScript to preprocess data and to check over it.

In this project, we will use JavaScript to process data without sending it to the server. In this case, we'll create a specialized calculator.

In developing this project, we'll learn about the following:

- Reading data from a web form

- Checking and verifying data

- Intercepting a form

- Coding a formula

- Storing data in the browser

Although we won't be submitting the form to a server (except to test the form), there's no reason why you can't do that as well, if, for example, you want to log inquiries, or do some further processing.

© Mark Simon 2023
M. Simon, *JavaScript for Web Developers*, https://doi.org/10.1007/978-1-4842-9774-2_6

Creating a Mortgage Repayment Calculator

A simple example of a specialized calculator is one which uses a specialized formula. Here, we will calculate the regular repayment given the principal (the amount borrowed), the interest rate, and the length of the mortgage.

You may or may not be passionately interested in financial calculations. Or you may be more interested in scientific calculations, or mathematical formulas. Of course, we're not so much focussed on the formula as on how to turn the formula into a form and how to implement that in JavaScript.

If you were to do this in a spreadsheet application, you'll probably find a built-in function called PMT() to do the same job. JavaScript doesn't have such a function, so you'll have to code it yourself.

If you have the time and mathematical knowledge, you may be able to derive the formula yourself. If you don't have the time or knowledge or inclination, you may be able to find a formula somewhere on the Internet.

Eventually, you'll find that the formula for repayment is

$$pr\frac{(1+r)^n}{(1+r)^n - 1}$$

where

- p = principal

- r = interest rate (per payment)

- n = number of payments

This will do the job, but two of the values are not very user-friendly. When calculating mortgages, we normally express the interest rate *per year*, not the rate *per payment*. And we normally work with the number of *years*, not the number of payments.

The most important rule in writing an application for humans is to let humans do what is natural to them and let the code make the adjustments necessary. *Never expect the user to make the adjustments: (a) they don't want to, (b) they'll probably make mistakes, and (c) they really don't want to.*

Part of the job, then, will be to convert from human-friendly values to formula-friendly values.

The Calculator Form

The data will come from the following form:

```
<form id="data">
    <fieldset>
        <p><label>Amount to be Borrowed:<br>
            <input type="text" name="principal"
                value="300000"></label></p>
        <p><label>Term in Years:<br>
            <input type="text" name="term" value="30">
            </label></p>
        <p><label>Frequency of Payment:<br>
            <input type="text" name="frequency"
                value="12"></label></p>
        <p><label>Interest Rate (% pa):<br>
            <input type="text" name="rate" value="6">
            </label></p>
    </fieldset>
    <fieldset id="results">
        <p><output name="result"></p>
        <p><button name="calculate">Tell Me</button></p>
    </fieldset>
</form>
```

It looks something like Figure 6-1.

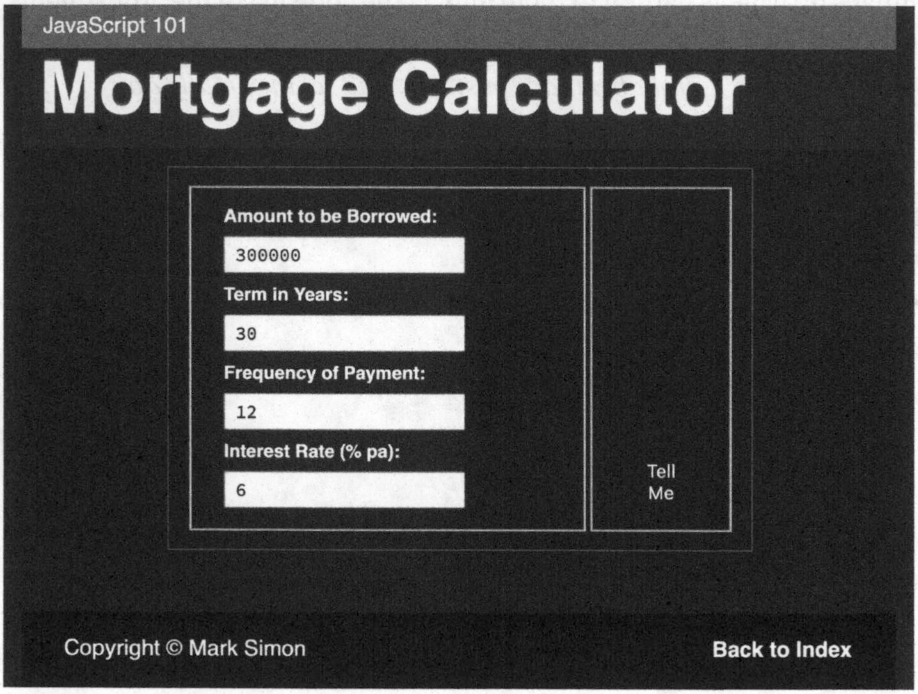

Figure 6-1. *The Mortgage Calculator form*

In this form, the two important input element types are `<input type="text" name="...">` and `<button name="...">`, which are the text boxes and action button.

You'll see that there's also an `output` element. That's a simple element into which you can write whatever you like in JavaScript. It will be part of the `elements` collection of the form, but if you were to submit the form, it wouldn't be included.

To implement the calculator, we will respond to the `button`, read and the process from the `input` elements, and place the result in the `output` element.

The Form Fields

The form fields are a user-oriented view of what values we need to process. They are

- `principal`: Amount to be borrowed

- `term`: Number of years for the mortgage

- `frequency`: Number of payments per year

- `rate`: Annual rate as a percentage

Note that these are all `text` type inputs. HTML does have a `type="number"`, but it's not so flexible. In any case, the data will be a string, even if we were to use `type="number"`, so there's not much benefit for us there.

The four values are the sorts of values a person would expect to fill in, but the formula wants something different. To prepare the values for the formula:

- The principal will remain the same.

- The interest rate per payment will be calculated as

  ```
  rate per payment
  = annual rate / payments per year / 100
  ```

  We divide by 100 to convert the percentage.

- Number of payments will be calculated as

  ```
  number of payments
  = term in years * payments per year
  ```

Note that we've made another concession to the user. We're used to expressing interest rates as a percentage, but JavaScript doesn't know anything about percentages. So we'll let the user type in what looks like a percentage, and we'll divide by 100 in the code.[1]

Initializing the JavaScript

The HTML code has already been prepared with the links to the JavaScript files:

```
<!DOCTYPE html>
<html lang="en">
    <head>
        ...
        <script type="text/javascript" src="scripts/library.js"
            crossorigin="anonymous"></script>
        <script type="text/javascript" src="scripts/calculator.js"
            crossorigin="anonymous" defer></script>
        ...
    </head>
    <body>
    ...
    </body>
</html>
```

Notice that this includes the library script. If some of the new code is reusable, we may want to move it to the library.

The `calculator.js` file has already been created for your convenience and is ready to go:

```
/*  Mortgage Calculator
```

---

[1] JavaScript does support the % operator, but it doesn't mean anything like percentage. It's used as a remainder after division.

182

```
=================================================== */
'use strict';
window.onerror=function(message,url,line) {
    alert(`Error: ${message}\n${url}: ${line}`);
};

doCalculator();

function doCalculator() {

}
```

We haven't bothered with a separate init() function, as there's nothing more to do there.

Processing the Form

The first step will be to locate the form and to reference it:

```
function doCalculator() {
    let calculatorForm = document.querySelector('form#data');
}
```

Having identified the form, you will need to attach an event listener to the submit button:

```
function doCalculator() {
    let calculatorForm = document.querySelector('form#data');
    calculatorForm.elements['calculate'].onclick = doit;

    function doit(event) {

    }
}
```

183

Here, the submit button has the name `calculate`. The event listener is the `doit` function. You might not think that `doit` is a very descriptive name, but we can justify its simplicity.

In this case, the `doit` function is **nested** inside the `doCalculator()` function. As a result, this function has a number of features:

- Being inside the `doCalculator()` function, the `doit` function inherits all of the outer variables. In this case, this will be the `calculatorForm` variable which will be important in getting the data values.

- As with local variables, nested functions are only accessible within the outer function, never from outside. You can call nested functions whatever you like without affecting the rest of your JavaScript.

  It is this feature which would justify a less descriptive name for the `doit` function, since it only has to make sense locally.

- The outer function is self-contained, as it includes all of its dependant functions, and there's no need to communicate with any other functions.

The `doit` function includes the `event` parameter, which we can use to stop the form from actually being submitted:

```
function doit(event) {
    event.preventDefault();
}
```

If you forget to do this, you will end up reloading your page every time you click the submit button, and you will never see your result.

Getting the Form Data Elements

There are four data elements to be used. You can use their values directly, but it will be easier to put them into variables:

```
function doit(event) {
    event.preventDefault();

    let principal = calculatorForm.elements['principal'].value;
    let term = calculatorForm.elements['term'].value;
    let frequency = calculatorForm.elements['frequency'].value;
    let rate = calculatorForm.elements['rate'].value;
}
```

There is nothing preventing the user from making errors, especially typing errors. The simplest error is extra spaces and one we can take in our stride using the trim() function:

```
function doit(event) {
    event.preventDefault();

    let principal =
        calculatorForm.elements['principal'].value.trim();
    let term = calculatorForm.elements['term'].value.trim();
    let frequency =
        calculatorForm.elements['frequency'].value.trim();
    let rate = calculatorForm.elements['rate'].value.trim();
}
```

The trim() function is applied to a string, in this case the .value property, and will remove any leading or trailing spaces. If there are other spaces inside the string, they will be unaffected.

Checking the Form Values

Remember, all form data starts off as a string, so you will need to make sure that it is converted to numbers. Although JavaScript will do this automatically if given the chance, it's better if you do it yourself. That way, you can also check for conversion errors. For example:

```
let principal = calculatorForm.elements['principal'].
value.trim();
    principal = parseFloat(principal);
```

The parseFloat() and parseInt() functions will both attempt to parse as much of a string as it can to a floating-point or integer number, starting from the beginning. If they encounter a character which would be invalid in a number, they stop parsing and use everything before that character. The difference between them is that parseFloat will also accept a decimal point, which would be invalid for an integer.

When you run a string through parseInt() or parseFloat(), there is always the possibility that the string fails conversion; that is, it's **invalid**. Checking whether the user data is valid is, of course, called **validation**. Modern HTML has some built-in validation for forms, but using JavaScript for this is more powerful.

If the string is empty or starts immediately with an invalid character, parseFloat() and parseInt() will result in NaN, a special value meaning "Not a Number." You can specifically test for this special value using one of two methods:

```
if(isNaN(principal)) ... ;          //  isNaN() function
if(principal != principal) ...   ;  //  NaN quirk
```

The first method uses the isNaN() function, which you need to remember has two capital Ns. The second method exploits an odd feature that NaN is not equal to anything, including NaN. You wouldn't use this method seriously, but you might like to show off.

In reality, you can just take advantage of the fact that NaN is treated as a falsy value, so you can just use the not (!) operator:

```
let principal = calculatorForm.elements['principal'].
value.trim();
    principal = parseFloat(principal);
    if(!principal) principal = 0;
```

This way, you can assign a default value if the string fails parsing.

In JavaScript, you can combine the last two steps shown previously using the || (or) operator:

```
let principal = calculatorForm.elements['principal'].
value.trim();
    principal = parseFloat(principal) || 0;
```

In JavaScript, the || operator is **short-circuited**. This means that if the first test is enough, the second won't be evaluated. In this case, if the first value is truthy, then the second won't be used, since the || only needs one success.

You can now preprocess the following values:

```
function doit(event) {
    event.preventDefault();

    let principal =
            calculatorForm.elements['principal'].value.trim();
        principal = parseFloat(principal);
        if(!principal) principal = 0;
    let term = calculatorForm.elements['term'].value.trim();
        term = parseFloat(term);
        if(!term) term = 0;
    let frequency =
            calculatorForm.elements['frequency'].value.trim();
```

```
        frequency = parseFloat(frequency);
        if(!frequency) frequency = 1;
    let rate = calculatorForm.elements['rate'].value.trim();
        rate = parseFloat(rate);
        if(!rate) rate = 0;
}
```

or more simply:

```
function doit(event) {
    event.preventDefault();

    let principal =
            calculatorForm.elements['principal'].value.trim();
        principal = parseFloat(principal) || 0;
    let term = calculatorForm.elements['term'].value.trim();
        term = parseFloat(term) || 0;
    let frequency =
            calculatorForm.elements['frequency'].value.trim();
        frequency = parseFloat(frequency) || 0;
    let rate = calculatorForm.elements['rate'].value.trim();
        rate = parseFloat(rate) || 0;
}
```

The default values all virtually do nothing except to provide harmless dummy values for the formula. You could easily have provided more meaningful values.

If you wanted to use the HTML default value, remember that HTML uses value for that attribute. However, JavaScript uses value for the current value, so you will need a different JavaScript property, defaultValue. For example:

```
principal = parseFloat(principal) ||
    parseFloat(calculatorForm.elements['principal'].
    defaultValue);
```

The continuation of that last statement is indented to make it easier to read.

Fixing the Form Values

Although some developers seem to make a sport of it, it's generally not a good idea to confuse your users. In this case, you may have adjusted some of the values, and you're about to use those adjusted values.

After you make any changes to the user's data, it's a good idea to put those values back into the form so that they can see what's actually going on. The value property of a form can be written as well as read, so we can write the adjusted values that way:

```
function doit(event) {
    event.preventDefault();

    let principal =
            calculatorForm.elements['principal'].value.trim();
        principal = parseFloat(principal) || 0;
        calculatorForm.elements['principal'].value = principal;
    let term = calculatorForm.elements['term'].value.trim();
        term = parseFloat(term) || 0;
        calculatorForm.elements['term'].value = term;
    let frequency =
            calculatorForm.elements['frequency'].value.trim();
        frequency = parseFloat(frequency) || 0;
        calculatorForm.elements['frequency'].value = frequency;
    let rate = calculatorForm.elements['rate'].value.trim();
        rate = parseFloat(rate) || 0;
        calculatorForm.elements['rate'].value = rate;
}
```

Although the .value property is technically a string and not a number, JavaScript knows that and will readily convert the number to a string.

You can try this out now with invalid values. Any defaulted values will be written back to the form, though, at this stage, nothing will be calculated yet.

Translating Mortgage Calculation

As we mentioned before, the formula for repayment is

$$pr\frac{(1+r)^n}{(1+r)^n-1}$$

The first thing you will have to do is to prepare the values for the value:

- The principal is straightforward, and we will use the value we have got from the form, `principal`. The only thing is that we might put it in a new variable for simplicity:

  ```
  let p = principle;
  ```

- The value n is the number of payments. Since we have the term in years (`term`) and the number of payments per year (`frequency`), the total number of payments is those two values, multiplied:

  ```
  let n = term * frequency;
  ```

- The value r is the interest rate *per payment*. Since we have an annual rate and the number of payments per year, we will have to divide the two. We will also have to divide by 100, since the number is supposed to be a percentage:

  ```
  let r = rate / frequency / 100;
  ```

We can now add the following to the function:

```
function doit(event) {
    event.preventDefault();

    ...

    let p = principal;
    let n = term * frequency;
    let r = rate / frequency / 100;
}
```

The next step is to convert the expression to JavaScript:

- The first part simply multiplies values, so you
  would write

  ```
  p * r * ...
  ```

- The expression (1+r)n means (1 + r) to the power of
  n. You can write this as

  ```
  (1 + r)**n
  ```

  In older JavaScript, you would have to write `Math.`
  `pow(1+r, n)`, using a built-in function to do the job.

- The expression $\frac{something}{something}$ means you will have to
  divide. However, the lower part of the expression
  is an addition, which you will need to enclose in
  parentheses.

Putting that together, the formula translates as

```
p * r * (1+r)**n / ((1+r)**n - 1)
```

Using older JavaScript, you would need

```
p * r * Math.pow(1+r,n) / (Math.pow(1+r,n) - 1)
```

Adding the code to the function:

```
function doit(event) {
    ...

    let repayment = p * r * (1+r)**n / ((1+r)**n - 1);
}
```

We'll save the result into a new variable, repayment.

Displaying the Results

Finally, we need to put the result onto the page. Remember the output element called result? We can write to it the same way that we write to the other form elements:

There is a paragraph whose id is results, so we'll need to locate it. We can call the variable result. We could do that within the doit function:

```
function doit(event) {
    ...

    let repayment = p * r * (1+r)**n / ((1+r)**n - 1);
    calculatorForm.elements['result'].value = repayment;
}
```

You may have noticed an excessive number of decimal places in the result. That's the result of dividing by a tricky number. You probably only want two decimal places.

Although JavaScript does have a rounding-off function (Math.round), it only rounds off to integers. In any case, *displaying* a number to a fixed number of decimal places is not the role of approximation functions. Rather, you should generate a *string* with whatever format you like.

Fortunately, JavaScript has a function that does the job: toFixed(...). This will convert a number to a string with the specified number of decimal places. We can simply apply this to the repayment variable:

```
function doit(event) {
    ...
    let repayment = p * r * (1+r)**n / ((1+r)**n - 1);
    calculatorForm.elements['result'].value = repayment.
    toFixed(2);
}
```

If you try this now with the default values, you should get a result of 1798.65.

Improvements

There are a few things we can do to make this calculator form a little better. Here, we'll do just these two things:

- Write the result in the local currency.
- Store the values locally for next time.

It's possible to get carried away with minor improvements, but these particular ones are not too difficult to implement.

Writing the Result in the Local Currency

If you're reading this anywhere but in Australia, it's possible that your local currency differs, and even how you represent decimals and long numbers may differ. It's actually very difficult to filter variations in input formats, but it's quite easy to output.

The Intl Object

JavaScript has a built-in object called `Intl`. It's very powerful – in fact, it's so powerful that it's a little tricky to work out how it works.

The `Intl` object is capable of formatting dates, times, and numbers according to one locale or another. It will even format lists according to custom. In our case, we're interested in formatting a number as a currency.

To use `Intl` formatting, you'll need to go through two steps. You can experiment in the console to get a feeling for how it works.

First, you create a new `NumberFormat` object, giving the locale, and how you want to treat the number:

```
»   var numberFormat = Intl.NumberFormat(
        'en-AU',
        { style: 'currency', currency: 'aud' }
    );
```

Here, the locale is set to en-AU, which means English in Australia. The important part here is that the locale helps define that the decimal is a dot (.) and thousands are separated by a comma (,). If you're doing this in Europe, say, you might want to use something like nl-NL, which is the format used in the Netherlands: the decimal and thousands characters are the other way round.

The second parameter is an options object. Here, we're saying that we want the number displayed as currency, using Australian Dollars. The currency and the locale don't have to match. If you want Australian Dollars displayed in the Netherlands number format, that's fine:

```
»   var numberFormat = Intl.NumberFormat(
        'nl-NL',
        { style: 'currency', currency: 'aud' }
    );
```

194

Formatting a Number

Of course, you won't get a formatted number yet. For that, you'll need the format() method of the object:

```
»    numberFormat.format(123456.789);
←    "$123,456.79"
```

Notice that the number has been rounded off correctly to two decimal places. Also notice that the result is a string. Numbers have a value only and don't include currency symbols or thousands separators. If you want that sort of embellishment, you need a string, which is fine for what we're going to do with it.

If you're going to use the formatter many times, you can make it a little more convenient if you include the format() method in the variable:

```
»    var format = Intl.NumberFormat(
         'en-AU',
           { style: 'currency', currency: 'aud' }
     ).format;
»    format(123456.789);
←    "$123,456.79"
```

Remember, in JavaScript, functions are data objects. You can assign a function as you might assign any other object. Here, we've assigned the format() method of the new NumberFormat object to a variable called format. We can use this variable as a function since that's what it contains.

We'll now add this to our code.

In principle, we could be recalculating many times. It would be wasteful to create a new formatting object every time, so we'll create it outside the doit() function:

```
function doCalculator() {
    let calculatorForm = document.querySelector('form#data');
    calculatorForm.elements['calculate'].onclick = doit;
```

```
let format = Intl.NumberFormat(
    'en-AU',
    { style: 'currency', currency: 'aud' }
).format;

function doit(event) {
    ...
}
}
```

We've changed the var to let because we're not in the console anymore.

The doit() function is, of course, run every time you click on the calculate button. As with the calculatorForm variable, it has access to the format() function from the containing function.

We won't need the toFixed() method anymore. That worked well enough, but the formatting function also rounds off the result. We can replace it with the following:

```
function doit(event) {
    ...
    let repayment = p * r * (1+r)**n / ((1+r)**n - 1);
    // calculatorForm.elements['result'].value =
    //     repayment.toFixed(2);
    calculatorForm.elements['result'].value =
    format(repayment);
}
```

That looks a little more professional.

The `Intl` object can do much more than formatting numbers. If you're interested in seeing what else you can do with it, you can go to `https://developer.mozilla.org/en-US/docs/Web/JavaScript/Reference/Global_Objects/Intl`.

Saving Values in Storage

This is a simple calculator with default values, so it's not much of a burden to the user. However, it's possible that remembering the values for next time may be appreciated.

You can't save data to the disk. That's by design, since a web page shouldn't be able to access the user's computer. You can, however, save some data to the browser's storage area.

In the past, saving data used browser cookies. That's actually a misuse of cookies. Here is how cookies were supposed to be used:

1. The user visits a site and possibly enters some data or searches for something.

2. The server responds with whatever has been requested, at the same time sending some additional data in the form of a cookie.

3. When the user visits the site again, any cookies associated with the site are returned to the server.

The process looks a little like Figure 6-2.

Figure 6-2. *Using cookies*

From the beginning, JavaScript has included the ability to read, modify, and even create cookies. These same cookies would be included when the browser revisits a server, even if they didn't originate there.

Using cookies for local storage has two major problems:

- All site-related cookies are sent to the server, even if they were created in JavaScript and didn't actually originate with the server. That means your data is never truly private.

- Manipulating cookies in JavaScript is actually quite tricky.

Using Web Storage

Thankfully, JavaScript now has a better mechanism for storing local data on the browser. This is known as **web storage** and has two forms:

- **Local storage** will be saved on the browser indefinitely.

  Local storage is available using a built-in object: `localStorage`.

- **Session storage** will be deleted automatically when the browser or tab is closed.

  Session storage is available using a built-in object: `sessionStorage`.

They both work the same way, so all you need to decide is how long you want the data to hang around. In this case, we'll use "localStorage".

The storage object has a number of methods to set and get data. Here, we'll store the values we have just used to calculate the result:

```
function doit(event) {
    ...
    // Store Values
    localStorage.setItem('data', true);
    localStorage.setItem('principal', principal);
    localStorage.setItem('term', term);
    localStorage.setItem('frequency', frequency);
    localStorage.setItem('rate', rate);
}
```

The actual names of the items can be whatever you like, of course, but here we've set them to the same names as the variables and the original form data.

We've also set another item, data. This will make it easy to test whether any data has been stored when we load the page the next time.

You can check what your browser has in storage in the Developer Tools. For Firefox and Safari, you'll find it in a Storage section. In Chromium, there's a Storage section in the Application section. You'll see something like this:

Key	Value
data	true
frequency	12
principal	300000
rate	6
term	30

The next part is to re-populate the values from storage. We do that when the page is loaded; that is when the doCalculator() function is run. Of course, that would only work if there are values saved from previously. That's where the data item comes in:

```
function doCalculator() {

  ...

  // Restore Values
     if(localStorage.getItem('data')) {

     }

   function doit(event) {

      ...

   }
}
```

The .getItem() method simply fetches a value by item name. If an item is not available, .getItem() returns a null, which, as we all know, is a falsy value. The if() statement checks whether it's truthy. We could have tested any of the other items for this, but it's easier to understand and maintain if we have a special value to check.

Restoring the items is tedious but simple. It's a matter of calling the .getItem() method for each of the values and putting these values into their corresponding form field:

```
function doCalculator() {

  ...

  // Restore Values
     if(localStorage.getItem('data')) {
         calculatorForm.elements['principal'].value =
             localStorage.getItem('principal');
         calculatorForm.elements['term'].value =
```

```
        localStorage.getItem('term');
    calculatorForm.elements['frequency'].value =
        localStorage.getItem('frequency');
    calculatorForm.elements['rate'].value =
        localStorage.getItem('rate');
    }

    ...

}
```

To try this out:

- Change some of the values and calculate the result.

- Go back to the home page.

- Now return to the calculator page and check whether the previous values have been restored.

The good thing about web storage is that it's not only easy to use, it's also secure. At least it's as secure as your browser is: if others can come up to your browser, they can still examine what was stored. For that reason, you should never store anything really sensitive this way.

At least it won't be sent back to the web server.

Using Array Processing

The part of the code that restores values includes a lot of repetition of code. Whenever there's code repetition, it may be possible to simplify it. In this case, the repetition involves doing the same thing with four items.

We can simplify this a little by putting the values in an items array:

```
['principal','term','frequency','rate']
```

To iterate through an array, we can use a counter loop. You can try this in the console:

```
»    var items = ['principal','term','frequency','rate'];
»    for(var i=0; i<items; i++) {
         console.log(item);
     }
```

In modern JavaScript, you can use an array method called `.forEach()`:

```
»    var items = ['principal','term','frequency','rate'];
»    items.forEach(function(item) {
         console.log(item);
     });
```

As you see, the `.forEach()` method takes a function with one or more parameters. The first, and most useful, parameter is each item of the array. While we're using modern JavaScript, it's also common to use an arrow function expression:

```
»    var items = ['principal','term','frequency','rate'];
»    items.forEach(item => {
         console.log(item);
     });
```

In an arrow function expression, the `item =>` replaces the `function(item)`. It's not much shorter, but it can be very concise for simple jobs.

We don't need to keep the data in a separate variable if we're going to use it immediately. You can apply the `.forEach()` method to an array literal:

```
»    ['principal','term','frequency','rate'].forEach(item => {
         console.log(item);
     });
```

We can use this to replace the part of the code that restores the values:

```
// Restore Values
   if(localStorage.getItem('data')) {
/*

      ...

*/

      ['principal','term','frequency','rate'].forEach(item => {
         calculatorForm.elements[item].value =
            localStorage.getItem(item);
      });
   }
```

The other code has been commented out while you test the new version. Once you've made sure the new code is working, you can delete the commented code.

Unfortunately, you can't really do the same thing with the code to store the values. That's because the data you want to store is in variables, and JavaScript has no simple way of iterating through normal variables.

Using an Object for Data

If you *really* want to iterate through the variables which we used in the calculator, there is an indirect way.

You have already met the Math object. It's basically a package of useful functions and data for mathematical work. You can readily make your own objects to do the same job.

We can try this in the console:

```
»   var data = {};
»   data.principal = 300000;
»   data.term = 30;
»   data.frequency = 12;
»   data.rate = 6;
```

In JavaScript, you can create a new object just by assigning an **object literal**, which is a collection of data contained in braces ({ ... }). In this case, the new object is an empty object.

From there, you can assign new properties and values, as you see in the example.

In the console, you can print out the object using `console.log()`:

»   `console.log(data);`

We can also combine this with the array iteration to list the contents of the object:

»   `['principal','term','frequency','rate'].forEach(item => {`
        `console.log(`$\`${item}: ${data[item]}\``);`
    `});`

We've used the template string literal to include the item name and the value from the `data` object.

Notice that we're using the square brackets notation for the object members. Remember that it's an alternative to the dot notation which allows us to use variables.

In our calculator code, we can replace instances of the four main variables with object properties. To begin with, we can fetch and check the data using a `.forEach()` loop:

```
function doit(event) {
    event.preventDefault();

    let data = {};

    ['principal','term','frequency','rate'].forEach(item => {
        data[item] = calculatorForm.elements[item].value.trim();
        data[item] = parseFloat(data[item]) || 0;
        calculatorForm.elements[item].value = data[item];
```

```
    });

    ...
}
```

The variables for the formula can then use these object properties instead of the old variables:

```
function doit(event) {
    event.preventDefault();
    ...
    let p = data.principal;
    let n = data.term * data.frequency;
    let r = data.rate / data.frequency / 100;
    ...
}
```

Finally, you can store the values the same way:

```
function doit(event) {
    event.preventDefault();
    ...
    ['principal','term','frequency','rate'].forEach(item => {
        localStorage.setItem(item, data[item]);
    });
}
```

The finished code would look like this:

```
function doit(event) {
    event.preventDefault();

    let data = {};

    ['principal','term','frequency','rate'].forEach(item => {
        data[item] = calculatorForm.elements[item].value.trim();
```

```
        data[item] = parseFloat(data[item]) || 0;
        calculatorForm.elements[item].value = data[item];
    });

    let p = data.principal;
    let n = data.term * data.frequency;
    let r = data.rate / data.frequency / 100;

    // Unaffected:
    let repayment = p * r * (1+r)**n / ((1+r)**n - 1);
    calculatorForm.elements['result'].value =
        format(repayment);

    // Store Values
    localStorage.setItem('data', true);

    ['principal','term','frequency','rate'].forEach(item => {
        localStorage.setItem(item, data[item]);
    });
}
```

Saving data in an object instead of separate variables is useful not only for iterating through the values. It can also simplify managing excessive variables and storing the data for later use. It's also a convenient way of packaging data to transfer between locations, such as getting data from a web server.

JavaScript has more recently added a **Map** object, which is more specifically designed to store data this way. However, it's not quite so convenient to use.

Summary

In this chapter, we had a look at processing data from a form and storing the data. To work through the idea, we developed a simple calculator to calculate mortgage repayments.

Getting Form Data

A web form includes an `elements` collection, which references all of the `input` and `output` elements. You can reference individual elements using either the "dot" or "square bracket" notation, but square brackets are more flexible and more consistent.

To reference an individual element, you can use an expression like `form.elements['...']`. However, this will get you the element itself; you probably really want the value in this element, using an expression like `form.elements['...'].value`.

All form data comes as strings. If you want to perform numeric processing, you should run the data through something like `parseInt()` or `parseFloat()`, which will parse the string as a number.

Data from a form is not guaranteed to be suitable, so you will need to check each value and possibly default to suitable values.

Normally, a form is expected to submit the data to an external process on the server. However, it's possible to intercept this using the `event.preventDefault()` method, which prevents the form's normal behavior. Sometimes, this is done conditionally, such as when the form data fails some sort of validation checks. In this case, the form was never meant to send data out.

Performing the Calculation

The whole point of a specialized calculator is to be able to run calculations that are otherwise too complex. Finding a suitable formula may need some research, and the formula is not always code-friendly.

The other problem is that sometimes the formula isn't human-friendly either. Part of the task is to take the sort of values that the user expects to be able to enter and to make the adjustments for the formula.

Finally, the formula may need translation to JavaScript expressions.

Displaying the Results

The output element allows you to set a value to be displayed on the form.

Sometimes, however, the calculated result is not yet in a suitable form, such as when there are too many decimal places to be meaningful. The .toFixed() method can format a number to a fixed number of decimal places. The result is actually a string, which is fine for outputting.

You can get a more flexible result using the Intl object, which can format numbers, as well as dates and other data, according to a particular locale and other preferences. In this case, we formatted the number as a currency for the locale. The result is also a string.

Storing the Data

JavaScript can't store data to the user's disk, but it can store data within the browser. In the past, this was done with cookies, though cookies weren't meant to be used that way.

Today we have access to web storage, which can be short term or longer term. This allows us to save values to be loaded next time the page is visited.

Since the storage object stores values with keys, we can use an array of key names and iterate through this array to simplify the repetition.

Plain variables can't be iterated this way, but we can create a simple object and store values in the object properties instead of using simple variables. The object properties can be referenced when iterating through an array of key names.

Coming Up

The next few projects will make some serious changes to what you see on the page. In some cases, we'll be creating new HTML elements; in some cases, we'll be showing and hiding them; and in some cases, we'll be constantly changing the content of these elements.

Before that, we need to learn a little more about manipulating the CSS styles, as well as how JavaScript responds to user events.

CHAPTER 7

Interacting with CSS and Event Listeners

In the slide show project, as well as the following projects, we rely on CSS to do much of the work. CSS, **Cascading Style Sheets**, is the language that mostly controls the appearance of the content of the page. You don't have to be an expert on CSS to make this work, but you should know some of the basic ideas so that you can understand what is going on and can easily make changes.

Here, we will look at

- The background of CSS

- What CSS can do

- Using event listener functions to react to a user event

- How we can interact with CSS using JavaScript

- Using JavaScript to create additional CSS styles

- CSS animation effects

You can experiment with both the CSS and JavaScript using your browser's development tools. There is a sample file, `sample-css.html`, for you to try things out, together with its CSS file `sample-css.css`.

The sample file looks like Figure 7-1.

© Mark Simon 2023
M. Simon, *JavaScript for Web Developers*, https://doi.org/10.1007/978-1-4842-9774-2_7

Figure 7-1. The CSS sample file

As we experiment with the ideas, especially with styles and event listeners, it's possible that the document starts to pick up some unwanted baggage. A page reload is your friend, so you can start afresh.

What Is CSS?

The original HTML didn't include any serious way of controlling the appearance of page content. An early attempt included the font element; the less said about that, the better.

Later the CSS language was developed. CSS controls the color, the font styles, the positioning, and even what is visible. It has developed to include some visual effects such as shadows, rounded corners, and the ability to control how solid an object is.

As CSS developed, it also added the ability to animate changes in these properties, either as simple transitions or as multi-stepped animations.

Some of these features, such as showing and hiding elements or animating their properties, have, in the past, been accomplished by JavaScript. In some of the projects, you will have added new elements to the document. If you keep adding and removing objects, you have a form of showing and hiding, but at the cost of a lot of extra coding and a lot of extra work for the browser as it has to cope with new and missing elements.

Similarly, we created a slide show, which shows one image after another. If you do this quickly enough, you have an animation, but again that means a lot of extra coding and work for the browser.

CSS now gives us the tools to do these things without writing them in JavaScript. What CSS doesn't do, however, is interact with the user or make decisions about when and how things happen. That's where JavaScript is needed.

Adding CSS in HTML

Typically, CSS is added in a separate CSS document and then linked using an HTML link element. You can see this in sample-css.html:

```
<link rel="stylesheet" type="text/css" href="styles/
sample-css.css"
    id="sample-css">
```

Here, the href attribute refers to the style sheet. In theory, as well as in practice, the href could be a full URL referencing a different site. The id isn't normally needed, but we'll be able to use it to achieve some effects later.

Styles can also be included in a style element in the HTML:

```
<style>
    /* style rules ... */
</style>
```

This is less manageable than an external style sheet, so it should be avoided under normal circumstances. However, there are times when you might need a custom style block in your page.

You can also create a style element in JavaScript, which would be the equivalent. You'll see more on creating a style element later.

Finally, you can assign styles to elements using the style attribute:

```
<p style="color: red">Hello</p>
```

This is called an inline style and is the most cumbersome way to do it. It's also hardest to override since it is applied after the other style sheets. However, once again, it can be useful to set this property in JavaScript.

Disabling Styles

You can disable a style block or a linked style sheet by setting a disabled attribute. You normally wouldn't do this in pure HTML, but you might use some JavaScript to turn this attribute on and off. That's one reason why the previous example includes an id attribute – to allow JavaScript to make changes to the link.

For example:

```
»    var link = document.querySelector('link#sample-css');
»    link.disabled = true;
```

You can activate the style sheet or block again by setting the property to false:

```
»    link.disabled = false;
```

Turning a style sheet on and off like this makes it possible, for example, to respond to user preferences. You might have an additional style sheet with a different font size or with different colors.

Event Listeners

Interacting with a web page involves setting up **event listeners**. An event listener is a function that will run in response to a user-generated event, such as clicking on something or pressing a key.

You can assign an event listener directly using an event property of the element. For example:

```
»    function doit() {
          console.log(h1.textContent);
     }
»    var h1 = document.querySelector('h1');
»    h1.onclick = doit;
```

Here, the event property is onclick, which will trigger when the user has clicked on the element. On touch-enabled devices, it will also respond to touching, so it's not necessarily a mouse-only event. When you click on the heading, or touch it, the function will print out the text of the heading.

As we've noted in previous chapters, don't think about writing the property as `onClick` or `onlick` or any other typographic variation.

If you want to remove the event listener, you can assign `null`:

```
»   h1.onclick = null;
```

You can also assign an event listener using `addEventListener`:

```
»   h1.addEventListener('click',doit);
```

The second method is clearly more complex, but it makes it possible to assign multiple event listeners and to change how it reacts with nested elements. There are also some events that don't have a simple `onsomething` version.

Since the `doit` function shown previously is specifically attached to the `h1` element, it seems repetitive to refer to `h1` again inside the function. For this, you need to know a little more about event targets.

If you want to remove an event listener added this way, you use `removeEventListener()`:

```
»   h1.removeEventListener('click',doit);
```

There is a trap in removing the event listener this way, which we'll see in the section on nested event listeners.

Using `.addEventListener()` is the preferred way of adding an event listener. However, in the following experiments, you are likely to be adding an event listener many times. This will result in many actions on a single event.

For each new section, be sure to remove the event listener previously added. Alternatively, you can reload the page.

Event Targets

When you trigger an event listener, you'll need to know what actually triggered it.

For example, in the sample file, there is a `figure` element with an image and a caption:

```
<figure>
    <img ...>
    <figcaption> ... </figcaption>
</figure>
```

You can assign an event listener to any of the elements shown previously, of course, but let's see what happens if you assign it to the `figure` element:

```
»    function doit(event) {
         console.log(this);
         console.log(event.target);
         console.log(event.currentTarget);
    }
»    var figure = document.querySelector('figure');
»    figure.addEventListener('click',doit);
```

The `doit()` function includes one parameter, `event`, which has the details of the event as well as methods to control it. Inside the function, there are three important values:

- `this` is a magic variable referring to the object holding the event listener function; in this case, it is the `figure` element.

- The `event.target` is the element that you actually clicked on.

- The event.currentTarget is the element that holds the
  event listener function; in *most* cases, it's the same as
  this, but not always.

If you click on the image or caption, you will get

```
<figure>
<img> or <figcaption>
<figure>
```

If you click on the space around the image, you'll get

```
<figure>
<figure>
<figure>
```

In all cases, this and event.currentTarget are the container, figure. The value of event.target depends on which element you actually click on.

Although writing this is clearly more convenient than event. currentTarget, its actual value will vary depending on how the function was called, so we'll stick to either event.currentTarget or event.target in future code.

The example in the previous section can now be written as

```
»   h1.removeEventListener('click', doit);   //  remove old
»   function doit(event) {
        console.log(event.target.textContent);
    }
»   var h1 = document.querySelector('h1');
»   h1.addEventListener('click', doit);
```

By replacing the h1 with event.target, you have made the event listener more reusable. You can also assign it to multiple elements and let the code work out which element you clicked on.

Nested Event Targets

You saw that clicking on the image also clicks on the containing figure element. That's by design, but not always what you want. Sometimes, you want to click on the image to stop there.

Before we do that, we need to understand how the click is propagated. When you click on an element nested inside another, the clicked element, as well as all of the containing elements, feels the click. The click is propagated in two phases. First, the click is felt from the outside in, from the outer elements to the inner element. This is called the **event capture** phase and is pictured in Figure 7-2.

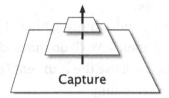

Figure 7-2. *Event capture*

It then reaches the **target** phase, which involves the element you actually clicked on.

After that, this click is felt from the inside out, from the inner element to the outer elements. This is called **event bubbling** and is pictured in Figure 7-3.

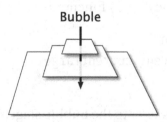

Figure 7-3. *Event bubble*

Most of the time, you're more interested in the bubble phase, starting with the clicked element.

When you use the direct `onclick` property, or the default `addEventListener()` method, the event listener will only respond to the bubble phase.

You can get the event listener to listen to the capture phase using the `addEventListener()` with an optional argument:

```
addEventListener('click', doit, true);
```

The third parameter can have other options, but using `true` indicates that it should listen to the capture phase; its default is `false`, which is why it defaults to the bubble phase.

You can test the bubbling and capturing phase by adding the same event listener to multiple elements. We'll do that with the figure and nested image. For this experiment, we'll use the `.currentTarget`, which will tell us which event listener is responding.

Before we do that, you need to make sure that the current event listener has been removed:

```
»    figure.removeEventListener('click',doit);
```

We'll also want a reference to the nested image:

```
»    var img = figure.querySelector('img');
```

Now, we'll redefine the `doit()` function:

```
»    function doit(event) {
          console.log(event.currentTarget);
     }
```

First, add the event listener to the bubble stage. This is the default, but we'll make the point by adding `false` as the last parameter:

```
»    figure.addEventListener('click', doit, false);
```

»   `img.addEventListener('click', doit, false);`

When you click on the image, you'll see that both elements call the event listener, but the img element responds first:

```
<img ...>
<figure>
```

Now remove the event listeners. When you remove an event listener, it must match the added event listener in event type (`click`), event listener function (`doit`), and listener type (`false`). If any of these is different, then the event listener won't be successfully removed. Since `false` is the default type, you don't need to specify it, but we'll do it anyway:

»   `figure.removeEventListener('click', doit, false);`
»   `img.removeEventListener('click', doit, false);`

Now, add them with the third argument to `true`, to call it in the capture phase:

»   `figure.addEventListener('click', doit, true);`
»   `img.addEventListener('click', doit, true);`

When you click on the image, you'll now see the responses in the reverse order:

```
<figure>
<img ...>
```

Again, to remove the event listener, you use `removeEventListener()`, matching all three arguments:

»   `figure.removeEventListener('click', doit, true);`
»   `img.removeEventListener('click', doit, true);`

In Chapter 8, we'll need to be aware of the propagation order of elements.

Stopping Propagation

You can stop the event function from processing any further. For example, you may decide that only the innermost element should be processed, or only the outermost element.

You can stop further processing with the stopPropagation() method. For example, if you want only the image to be processed, you can use

```
»   function doit(event) {
        event.stopPropagation();
        console.log(event.currentTarget);
    }
»   figure.addEventListener('click', doit, false);
»   img.addEventListener('click', doit, false);
```

If you click on the image now, you'll get only the image, which is the innermost element, in the output. You can now remove the event listeners again:

```
»   figure.removeEventListener('click', doit, false);
»   img.removeEventListener('click', doit, false);
```

If you wanted only the figure element to respond, you would use the capture phase by setting the third parameter to true.

Making Direct Changes to CSS Styles

JavaScript can directly access an element's CSS styles using the style property of the element. For example:

```
»   var h1 = document.querySelector('h1');
»   h1.style.color = 'red';
```

Setting the `style` property is similar to using inline styles in HTML:

```
<h1 style="color: red">This is a heading</h1>
```

You can read the property set this way:

```
»    h1.style.color
←    red
```

However, you can only read a property this way if it was set directly. Properties set in normal CSS can't be read this way.

As with inline styles, the `style` property is applied after all the other styles, so you can't override this with other CSS style sheets. This is OK for some simple properties, but not very flexible, and later you will see how to cooperate with style sheets better.

The `styles` property is an **object**, which is itself a package of data with its own properties. JavaScript has two ways of addressing a property:

```
»    var h1 = document.querySelector('h1');

»    h1.style.color = 'red';          //  dot notation
»    h1.style['color'] = 'green';     //  square brackets
```

The first notation, often called the **dot notation** for obvious reasons, is clearly simpler, but it has some limitations. The second notation, the so-called **square brackets notation** for equally obvious reasons, overcomes these limitations.

The first limitation, which is most apparent with CSS, is that the dot notation doesn't allow property names, which would be invalid names in JavaScript. For example, the `background-color` property includes a hyphen, which is disallowed in JavaScript since it would be interpreted as subtraction. Here, the square brackets notation comes to the rescue:

```
»    var h1 = document.querySelector('h1');
```

```
»   h1.style.background-color = 'yellow';        //  Error
»   h1.style['background-color'] = 'orange';      //  Valid
»   h1.style.backgroundColor = 'purple';          //  camelCase
```

As you see here, hyphenated CSS properties may be replaced with a camelCase alternative. However, for consistency with standard CSS, we will prefer the square brackets notation.

The second limitation of the dot notation is that the property name is hard-coded. You can't use a variable for the property. The square brackets notation, on the other hand, lets you use a variable instead of a string literal.

You might be wondering why you would use JavaScript to change the color at all, since it should have been set in CSS. The reason is that CSS sets the property once, while JavaScript can be used to interact with the user, so you can easily set it to something else.

For example, you can toggle the heading's color this way:

```
»   var h1 = document.querySelector('h1');
»   function doit(event) {
        if(event.target.style['color'] != 'yellow')
            event.target.style['color'] = 'yellow';
        else event.target.style['color'] = 'orange';
    }
»   h1.addEventListener('click',doit);
```

There is some repetition in this code. We can improve on this, but that calls for a minor detour.

Resetting Properties

If you want to remove a property set this way, you can set it to null or to an empty string(''):

```
»   h1.style['color'] = null;                   //  or ''
»   h1.style['background-color'] = null;    //  or ''
```

This will allow the element to fall back on the properties set previously in CSS.

While we're at it, we should also remove the event listener:

```
»   h1.removeEventListener('click',doit);
```

If we don't remove the event listener, all of our additional experiments will pile on more event listeners, and the element will respond in multiple ways.

Setting colors this way is probably not such a good idea, since you would rather make the artistic decisions elsewhere. However, the technique can be used to show or hide elements, as you'll see in the following projects.

If you want JavaScript to change some of the more artistic properties, you can use the techniques in the sections on using classes and style sheets.

Storing State

In the previous example, we tested whether a color had already been set before deciding what to do with it. Apart from the tediousness, the technique hard-codes too many values.

A better technique would be to store what we've done in a separate variable. We'll call that a **state** variable.

One simple method is to create a variable outside the function and test and set it inside the function:

```
»   var h1 = document.querySelector('h1');
»   var modified = false;
»   function doit(event) {
```

225

```
        if(!modified) event.target.style['color']
            = 'yellow';
        else event.target.style['color'] = null;
        modified = !modified;
    }
» h1.addEventListener('click',doit);
```

When you've finished testing, remove the event listener:

```
» h1.removeEventListener('click',doit);
```

We can improve on the code shown previously. If you're setting a value based on a test, you can simplify the process.

Conditional Operators

JavaScript has a **conditional operator** (a.k.a. **ternary** operator), which combines a test with a choice of values. For example:

```
» var a = 3, b = 4;
» a == b ? 'yes' : 'no';
← "no"
```

The conditional operator has three parts. The first part is the test. You can use any expression you might have used in an if() or while() statement. The second part is the value if the test is true or truthy. The third part is the value if not.

We can rewrite the previous code using the conditional operator:

```
» var h1 = document.querySelector('h1');
» var modified = false;
» function doit(event) {
        event.target.style['color'] =
            !modified ? 'yellow' : null;
```

```
    modified = !modified;
  }
```

» `h1.addEventListener('click',doit);`

Not only is this simpler, it makes the intention clearer.

When you've finished testing, remove the event listener:

» `h1.removeEventListener('click',doit);`

Static Variables

At some point, you'll probably hear that JavaScript doesn't support static variables, and technically, that's correct.

In languages that do support static variables, it means that it's possible for a function variable to retain its value between calls. For example, you might have something like this:

» `// This doesn't work:`
» ```
function test() {
    static var value;
    value = value ? value+1 : 1;
    console.log(value);
}
```
» `test();`
» `test();`
» `test();`

As you see from the comment, it won't work in JavaScript. That's because JavaScript really doesn't support static variables. However, you can *emulate* static variables if you take advantage of the fact that all JavaScript functions are technically objects. That means they have properties, and you can add more properties if you like.
```

To make the previous sample work, we change the value variable into a .value property of the function:

```
»    function test() {
         test.value ??= 0;          // undefined → 0
         test.value ++;
         console.log(test.value);
     }
»    test();
»    test();
»    test();
```

If you attempt to read a nonexistent property, such as test.value, the first time around, you'll get undefined, which, remember, is not an error unless you attempt to use it in a calculation. The first time round, you'll need to check this and, if it is undefined, give it a real value.

You can use a statement like this:

```
»    if(test.value === undefined) test.value = 0;
```

You need the identity operator (===) to avoid confusing undefined with other falsy values. However, it's much simpler, and more readable when you get used to it, to use the shorter expression shown previously.

In JavaScript, this is the **nullish coalescing operator** that tests the first value specifically for null or undefined, which, among other things, avoids the confusion. You can test it like this:

```
»    undefined ?? 23
←    23
```

You can combine it with an assignment operator to create the **nullish coalescing assignment operator** (??=).

We can use the same technique to dispense with the state variable in the event listener:

```
»   var h1 = document.querySelector('h1');
»   //  var modified = false;   //  not needed
»   function doit(event) {
        doit.modified ??= false;
        event.target.style['color'] =
            !doit.modified ? 'yellow' : null;
        doit.modified = !doit.modified;
    }
»   h1.addEventListener('click',doit);
```

This makes the function more self-contained since it doesn't rely on an external variable to maintain state.

When you've finished testing, remove the event listener:

```
»   h1.removeEventListener('click',doit);
```

Dynamic CSS Changes

Because you now have JavaScript heavily involved, you can vary the style in more interesting ways. For example, this will change the background color at random:

```
»   var h1 = document.querySelector('h1');
»   var colours
        = ['red','orange','yellow','green','blue','violet'];
»   function doit(event) {
        //  random index
        var i = Math.floor(Math.random() * colours.length);
        event.target.style['background-color'] = colours[i];
    }
»   h1.addEventListener('click',doit);
```

The `colours` variable is simply an array of color names. The variable `i` is a random number that will be used as an index to the array. When you click on the heading, its background color will be set to a random color.

That's certainly something that CSS can't do by itself.

When you've finished testing, remove the event listener:

```
» h1.removeEventListener('click',doit);
```

If you don't like the color you ended with, you can also remove it:

```
» h1.style['background-color'] = null;
```

Reading Other CSS Properties

If you're going to start tampering with individual CSS properties, you'll lose the original CSS settings that have been so carefully and lovingly added to the page. You can read these properties, perhaps with a view to restoring your changes.

For example, we can toggle the heading background color to between a new color and the original, whatever that is.

If you've been following along, you may find yourself piling up event listeners. At this point, if you reload the page, all of this will be cleared.

To read all of the available CSS properties of an element, you can use `window.getComputedStyle(element)`, or `getComputedStyle(element)` for short. For example:

```
» var h1 = document.querySelector('h1');
» var styles = getComputedStyle(h1);
» console.log(styles['background-color']);
```

The result of `getComputedStyle(element)` is an object that includes all of the CSS properties applied to the element, whether they have been inherited or deliberately set, or, more likely, both. In this case, we want the `background-color` property, which was set in the `styles.css` style sheet.

We can store this in a variable and use it for our toggle:

```
var h1 = document.querySelector('h1');
var styles = getComputedStyle(h1);
var originalColour = styles['background-color'];
function doit(event) {
    doit.modified ??= false;
    event.target.style['background-color'] =
        !doit.modified ? 'yellow' : originalColour;
    doit.modified = !doit.modified;
}
h1.addEventListener('click',doit);
```

Generally, it's always a good idea to take note of the original CSS properties if you're going to make changes to them in JavaScript.

Don't forget to remove the event listener, as well as the color, for future experiments. Alternatively, you can just reload the page.

```
h1.removeEventListener('click',doit);
h1.style['background-color'] = null;
```

Working with the CSS Style Sheet

The main problem with making direct changes to styles is that the decisions are made in JavaScript and implemented by the JavaScript developer. In many cases, these are artistic decisions and should be made by the designer in CSS. Even if the two roles are taken by the same human, you should separate JavaScript logic from the artistic styles.

The simplest approach is to set all of the styles in the CSS style sheet and use a class to distinguish between alternative states. Then you would change the class value in JavaScript.

For example, in the `sample-css.css` style sheet, you would find something like this:

```
h1.different-color {
    color: #dac1a4;
}
h1.different-background {
    background-color: #587272;
}
```

You'll notice that there are two different classes, each with their own property. If you wanted either class to be applied, you could add the following in HTML:

```
<h1 class="different-color"> ... </h1>
```

You can even add multiple classes:

```
<h1 class="different-color different-background"> ... </h1>
```

However, that only works if you wanted that to be permanent. If you wanted to change the class dynamically, you can do it in JavaScript:

»   `var h1 = document.querySelector('h1');`
»   `h1.className = 'different-color';`

If you want to apply multiple classes, you can just list them:

»   `var h1 = document.querySelector('h1');`
»   `h1.className = 'different-color different-background';`

Most element properties in JavaScript have the same name as their corresponding attributes in HTML, but not the class name. That's because `class` has a special meaning in JavaScript, so JavaScript uses `className` to avoid the conflict.

You can remove a class by setting `className` to an empty string.

```
h1.className = '';
```

Managing more than one class in a string like this can be tricky if you want to work with them individually. Modern JavaScript now has an alternative way of manipulating classes using `.classList`:

```
»   var h1 = document.querySelector('h1');
»   h1.classList.add('different-color','different-background');
```

You can add as many classes as you like this way, but it's usually used with a single class.

You then remove the class to revert its style:

```
»   var h1 = document.querySelector('h1');
»   h1.classList.remove('different-color');
```

The `classList` property allows you to manipulate one class at a time, leaving the others intact. The `classList` property also gives you more control, as it has the following methods:

- `.classList.add(...)` adds the class if it isn't there already, or ignores it if it is.

  You can have multiple classes in the list.

- `.classList.remove(...)` removes the class if it is there, or ignores it if it isn't.

  You can have multiple classes in the list.

- `.classList.toggle(...)` adds the class if it isn't there already, or removes it if it is.

  `.classList.toggle()` can have a second parameter. If it's `true`, it will add the class, and if it's `false`, it will remove it.

- .classList.contains(...) tells you whether the element has the class.

You will find the .classList.toggle() method particularly useful. For example, you can use it in a click event handler:

```
»    var h1 = document.querySelector('h1');

»    function toggle(event) {
         event.target.classList.toggle('different-color');
     }

»    h1.addEventListener('click',toggle);
```

When you've finished, you can remove the event listener:

```
»    h1.removeEventListener('click',toggle);
```

A Note on Event Listener Function Expressions

Notice in the previous example that you have defined a function purely to assign it as an event listener. That might be regarded as a formality since the event listener must be a function, but you won't actually read to refer the function again.

You can simplify that by assigning the event listener function directly. If you use the onclick event property, you can write

```
»    var h1 = document.querySelector('h1');

»    h1.onclick = function(event) {
         event.target.classList.toggle('different-color');
     };
```

Here, we use a **function expression** that is basically a function that hasn't been defined separately. It is particularly useful if you're going to assign it immediately.

Modern JavaScript has an alternative syntax for function expressions:

```
»   var h1 = document.querySelector('h1');

»   h1.onclick = event => {
        event.target.classList.toggle('different-color');
    };
```

This is called an **arrow function** expression and is very often used in Modern JavaScript for assigned functions. However, there is one trap when using arrow functions.

Earlier, you saw that you can use the this keyword to refer to the element with the event listener. This won't work with arrow functions, as arrow functions do not associate this with different objects. That's one reason why it's better to use the event.target property.

If you want to use the .addEventListener method, it works the same way, but the function expression is added inside the parentheses, making it a little harder to follow.

For example, using the classic function expression:

```
»   var h1 = document.querySelector('h1');

»   h1.addEventListener('click', function(event) {
        event.target.classList.toggle('different-color');
    });
```

or using an arrow function expression:

```
»   var h1 = document.querySelector('h1');

»   h1.addEventListener('click', event => {
        event.target.classList.toggle('different-color');
    });
```

This is slightly harder to read, but it allows the flexibility you get with the .addEventListener() method.

The real problem is that the event listener is now anonymous, and you can't easily remove it, since you don't have a direct reference to it. There are two workarounds.

First, you can name the anonymous function as a property of the element:

```
»   var h1 = document.querySelector('h1');

»   h1.addEventListener('click', h1.fn = function(event) {
        event.target.classList.toggle('different-color');
    });
```

This works better with classic (non-arrow) function expressions, because of the operator precedence of arrow function expressions. Here, the function expression is at the same time assigned to h1.fn, or whatever property name you want to give it.

To remove the event listener, you can use the h1.fn property:

```
»   h1.removeEventListener('click', h1.fn);
```

The second method is much more drastic, but an excellent way of clearing out the accumulated event listeners:

```
»   h1.outerHTML = h1.outerHTML;
```

The outerHTML property is basically the HTML of the element itself. What you're doing here is basically reconstructing the element. This doesn't include any JavaScript but will include any classes that have been added to it.

You can use the outerHTML method if you've started to lose track of your added event listeners and you really don't want to reload your page.

Triggering a CSS Transition

A CSS **transition** is a gradual change from one style to another, such as changing an element's color, size, or opacity. You can regard it as a simple one-off animation. This relies on two parts:

- First, there must be a setting that defines *which* properties are to be transitioned and how long to take.

- Second, there must be two different values for a property. One of the values may be a default, such as black for text color.

For simple CSS transitions, you can use straight CSS, but for more complex behavior, you can use JavaScript.

A Simple CSS Transition

You can implement transitions in CSS, but CSS doesn't respond to user actions very well. As a result, you normally see them as a result of moving the mouse over an element, such as when a button changes color.

For example, when you hover the mouse over the sample button, its coloring changes. Here's the part of the CSS that causes that:

```
button#sample-button {
    ...

    background-color: rgb(0,34,34);
```

```
    color: white;
    transition: color 0.5s, background-color 0.5s
}

button#sample-button:hover {
    color: rgb(0,34,34);
    background-color: white;
}
```

The transition is triggered by hovering the mouse, because that's about all you can do in straight CSS. You can also sometimes respond to a click, but CSS isn't very cooperative that way.

You'll also notice that the change takes about half a second, which is good. That's because of the transition property.

Transitioning in JavaScript

In the Old Days, all transitions and animations were implemented in JavaScript. That's because CSS didn't know how. Whole libraries were built around transitions and animations, and some are used even today. Most of the time, we don't need them anymore.

If you really want to implement your own JavaScript transition, you can use a modified version of the code used in the slide show project. A transition is simply a fast repetition of changes.

Here is how you might use JavaScript to fade out the image element in 20 steps:

```
»   var img = document.querySelector('figure>img');
    var i = 0;
»   function fading() {
        img.style.opacity = 1 - i/20;
        i++;
        if(i>20) clearInterval(timer);
```

```
      }
»   var timer = setInterval(fading, 100);
```

If you want to take this seriously, you can wrap this in a function:

```
»   function fade(element, time, steps=20) {
        var interval = time/steps;
        var i = 0;
        var timer = setInterval(fading, interval);
        function fading() {
            element.style.opacity = 1 - i/steps;
            i++;
            if(i>steps) clearInterval(timer);
        }
    }
»   fade(document.querySelector('figure>img'), 2000, 20);
```

Here, the image is now passed as a parameter, and the total time (2000 milliseconds) and the number of steps are also passed; inside the function, they are used to calculate the interval for the setInterval() function and the increment for the opacity.

However, *we really don't want to do this*, especially where other more complex transitions are involved. Thankfully, CSS comes to the rescue.

A JavaScript CSS Transition

You can also implement transitions in JavaScript by setting the CSS properties and triggering the changes with event listeners.

For example:

```
»   var h1 = document.querySelector('h1');
»   // Initial Properties
»       h1.style.transition = 'border-color 3s';
»       h1.style['border'] = 'thick solid';
```

```
»        h1.style['border-color'] = 'red';

»    function doTransition(event) {
           doTransition.modified ??= false;
           event.target.style['border-color'] =
               !doTransition.modified ? 'yellow' : 'red';
           doTransition.modified = ! doTransition.modified;
       }
»    h1.onclick = doTransition;
```

When you click on the heading, the border color will eventually change to yellow, but it will take three seconds to do so. Clicking on it again will change it back to red.

The transition effect requires two things:

- A transition property is set on the border-color property.

- The border-color property is then changed.

This is *much* better than relying on the :hover pseudoclass, since the change is only implemented when the user specifically wants it. The world would be a slightly better place if pop-up menus did that instead of suddenly appearing from nowhere when the user moves a mouse.

If you try to change the property twice in a row, you will run into a few problems:

```
»    var h1 = document.querySelector('h1');

»    h1.style['transition'] ='border-color 3s';
»    h1.style['border-color'] = 'red';
»    h1.style['border-color'] = 'yellow';
```

The problem is that the browser won't wait around for the three seconds to complete the color change before it changes it again. Instead, it will take a shortcut and just assign the second value.

If the element was a different color to begin with, you will only see a transition to the second color. If the element was already the second color, you won't see anything at all.

JavaScript doesn't like to be kept waiting, but you can get it to come back to a task when the time comes. In this case, you can assign a function to run when the transition has ended. This requires responding to the transitionend event:

```
»   var h1 = document.querySelector('h1');

»   h1.style['transition'] = 'border-color 3s';
»   h1.ontransitionend = event => {
        event.target.style['border-color'] = 'yellow';
    };
»   h1.style['border-color'] = 'red';
```

These examples have all used color as an obvious property to test with. You can also use this technique with opacity:

```
»   h1.style.transition='opacity 4s';
»   h1.ontransitionend = event => {
        event.target.style['opacity'] = 1;
    }

»   h1.style.opacity = 0;
```

... or with size:

```
»   h1.style['overflow']='hidden';

»   h1.style.transition='max-height 4s';
»   h1.style['max-height'] = '2em';
»   h1.ontransitionend = event => {
        event.target.style['max-height'] = '2em';
```

```
       }
»      h1.offsetHeight;
»      h1.style['max-height'] = '0';
```

That last example needed some additional style changes to make the transition more obvious. The overflow property controls what happens if the content doesn't fit in the box. In this case, the content is hidden instead of overflowing.

It also needed a few tricks to make it work:

- A transition only takes place if the property is actually changed. That's why the max-height property was initially set to 2em.

- JavaScript will also impatiently combine the two max-height settings if it's allowed to. Before setting it the second time, we included h1.offsetHeight to force a screen update.

Triggering a CSS transition in JavaScript is a little tricky, as you can see, but it is still much simpler than attempting to do the whole transition in JavaScript. In the next section, you'll see how you can defer more of the artistic work to CSS itself.

Creating Style Sheets in JavaScript

In the discussion earlier on using classes, you will notice a dependence on an existing CSS style sheet. Of course, the fine details of how your page elements appear should be left to the style sheet and its developer, but there are some techniques in JavaScript that will become fragile if it relies on somebody else doing their job.

In cases where the JavaScript code absolutely requires some CSS properties, it is better for JavaScript to set these properties. It is even better if JavaScript can set these properties in such a way as to allow the CSS developer to override them with preferred values.

Creating the Style Sheet

If you were to define styles in the HTML itself, you would create a style element:

```
<head>
    <style>
        ...
    </style>
    ...
    <link rel="stylesheet" href="...">
    ...
</head>
```

The style element would contain additional styles for this page only. Note that in this example, it is placed *before* the link element, which loads an external style sheet. It could have been placed after, but being placed before allows the external style sheet to override the internal styles.

It is generally a bad idea to define styles this way in the HTML because it is harder to maintain, but we will use a variation of this technique in JavaScript.

To create a style sheet in JavaScript, we use document. createElement(), which can be used to create any HTML element at all:

```
»   var style = document.createElement('style');
»   document.head.insertAdjacentElement('afterbegin', style);
```

The variable `style` is used to add the element to the document and will also be used later to add CSS rules.

To add the style element to the `head` element, the easiest method is to use `insertAdjacentElement`, which allows you to add the new element inside or outside, at the beginning or end, of the original element.

Note that the new style sheet is added at the beginning of the `head` element, before any other style sheets that have already been added. This allows the linked style sheets to override properties if desired.

Adding CSS Rules

You can now add your CSS rules using the `insertRule()` function with a string of CSS:

```
»    style.sheet.insertRule(`h2 {
         border: medium solid white;
         border-style: none none solid none;
         padding-bottom: 0.5em;
     }`);
```

CSS can be written as a single line, but you normally have line breaks between the properties to make the code more manageable. That's why we used the template string literal to allow line breaks in the string.

In this example, we added some CSS that could readily have been included in one of the standard style sheets, so it's a bit wasted here. However, in Chapter 9, on the Lightbox, we'll be using this technique to add some essential CSS that is required to make the effect work. By putting the new style sheet at the beginning, you still have the option of overriding some of the properties with regular style sheets.

Summary

In this chapter, we explored working with CSS styles and JavaScript event listeners.

CSS

CSS is the standard way of adding styling to a web page. It can be added to HTML as a style block but is more usually added as a link to a separate style sheet. It is also possible to add CSS styles directly to individual elements using a `style` attribute.

You can make CSS style changes to elements using JavaScript, either by adding the styles directly or by changing the element classes associated with styles.

JavaScript can also selectively disable or enable individual style sheets.

Event Listeners

An event listener is a function set up to respond to a user event, such as using the mouse or keyboard.

You can add event listeners to elements either through event listener properties such as `.onclick` or with the `.addEventListener()` method. The `addEventListener()` method is more flexible and allows multiple event listeners to be added to a single element.

Event listeners can also be removed.

An event listener does not need to be a full function. It can be a function expression, which is a function that is not stored separately. It can also be an arrow function expression, which is a simplified version. However, using a function expression makes it trickier to remove.

Event listener functions have access to an event object, which contains information about the event that has just occurred. One important property of the event object is the `target`, which refers to the element that triggered the event.

The same event listener function can be used for multiple elements. If the elements are nested, all events will experience the event, both in the capture stage, which is from the outside in, and in the bubble stage, which is from the inside out.

Changing CSS Properties and Classes

Individual CSS properties can be changed using the element's `style` object. CSS properties can be accessed like any other object property, but we use the square brackets notation so that the properties could be consistent with CSS property names.

It's also possible to change CSS styles indirectly by changing the element's class or classes. This allows the CSS styles to be set in the style sheet, leaving JavaScript to trigger the changes.

Classes can be set using the `.className` property, but using the `.classList` object is more flexible.

It's also possible to read all of the styles applied to an element which have been added directly, through a style sheet, or inherited. This is useful in restoring any changes you might have made.

Toggling Properties

One common application of JavaScript is to change properties back and forth – to toggle them.

It can be useful to store the current state in a variable. This can be done in a variable outside the function, or as a property of the function object, acting as a kind of static variable.

A nullish coalescing operator can be used to initialize a variable. A conditional operator can be used to toggle between two states.

Transitions

A transition is a gradual change in the CSS style. In the past, this would have been accomplished in JavaScript using repeated calls to a function, in a similar way to the JavaScript slide show code. Modern CSS can handle these transitions without extra JavaScript.

You can trigger a CSS transition by setting the `transition` property in JavaScript and changing the affected CSS property. Alternatively, you can trigger a transition by changing the class using a predefined transition.

Creating Style Sheets

Under normal circumstances, all CSS should be implemented in the attached style sheets. However, there may be a requirement for additional styles. This can be achieved by creating a new style element in JavaScript and adding it to the document.

Coming Up

The next two projects will put all of this into practice. Chapter 8 focuses on how JavaScript can toggle the visibility of certain elements by toggling classes.

Chapter 9 focuses on creating new elements, adding CSS styles, hijacking HTML anchors, and more on event listeners, including working with the keyboard.

CHAPTER 8

Showing and Hiding Content

Something you will very often see on web pages is sections that open and close. They may be menu items or sections of content.

In this project, we'll toggle both content and lists. The technique is similar, which is a matter of having JavaScript change the state of a selected element. For the rest, we will allow CSS to do the job of showing and hiding content, as well as adding a little animation for good measure.

The page we're working with will be in the **Varying Content** link and is called showing-hiding.html. To begin with, the page looks like Figure 8-1.

© Mark Simon 2023
M. Simon, *JavaScript for Web Developers*, https://doi.org/10.1007/978-1-4842-9774-2_8

Figure 8-1. *Varying Content*

The content sections and the lists are closed. There rest of the content is there, but it's hidden in CSS. We'll write code to change that.

For good measure, there's also a section at the end that discusses changing the behavior of radio buttons based on a technique we'll develop in the first exercise on content headings.

The Initial HTML and JavaScript

The page `showing-hiding.html` has already been set up with the content and the links to the JavaScript:

```
<script type="text/javascript" src="scripts/library.js"
    crossorigin="anonymous"></script>
<script type="text/javascript" src="scripts/showing-hiding.js"
    crossorigin="anonymous" defer></script>
```

Again, we've included the library in the event we write something reusable. And, again, there's no defer attribute for that since there's nothing to run immediately.

The JavaScript file showing-hiding.js has also been set up:

```
init();

function init() {
    doHeadings();
    doMenu();
    doForm();
}

function doHeadings() {

}

function doMenu() {

}

function doForm() {

}
```

The init() function will call *three* functions, for the separate parts of this project.

Showing and Hiding Text Content

This part of the project will allow you to show and hide blocks of text, using their headings as a toggle.

The Basic HTML

The basic format of the content is something like this:

```
<div id="headings">
    <h2> ... </h2>
    <div>
        <!-- content -->
    </div>
    <h2> ... </h2>
    <div>
        <!-- content -->
    </div>
</div>
```

The whole of the content is inside a div element. Often divs are used to control layout, but here the div is used as a main container.

Since a div has no specific default behavior, other than as a block element, it is normal to give it an id or a class to identify it. In this case, the id is headings, and the container is identified as div#headings. This is used in both CSS and JavaScript.

There are more div elements, but they are easily identified as being inside the main div. The same also goes for the h2 elements, which normally define headings but will also be used to show and hide the content.

The purpose of the inner div elements is to contain the content to be shown or hidden after the heading. In CSS, they are identified as h2+div, which means a div *after* an h2.

Using this one id, we can identify the main container and its contents using the following selectors:

Elements	Selector
Main Container div	div#headings
Inner h2	div#headings>h2
div after h2	div#headings>h2+div

Note that we've tried to minimize the requirements on the HTML. The container must have an id, and the content must follow a pattern. That's all.

Preparing the Toggle Code

The first thing we need to do is find the headings that will toggle the appearance of the divs.

JavaScript has two functions that locate elements using a CSS selector. The querySelector() function finds the *first* match and is particularly useful if you know that the element is supposed to be unique. The querySelectorAll() function returns a numbered collection of matches. For this project, we'll use querySelectorAll().

If there isn't a match for querySelectorAll(), you will get an empty collection. The simplest way to test for an empty collection is to test its length.

To fetch all of the headings, we can use

```
function doHeadings() {
    let headings = document.querySelectorAll('div#headings>h2');
    if(!headings.length) return;
}
```

The collection will be stored in the headings variable. If there was no match, the length is 0, which is falsy, and the function will return immediately since there's nothing else to do.

If there's any thought of making this code reusable, we should remove the hard-coded reference to div#headings and make that a parameter variable. We'll still need the h2 part of it, so we'll put them together in a template string literal:

```
function doHeadings(container) {
    let headings = document.querySelectorAll(`${container}>h2`);
    if(!headings.length) return;
}
```

We'll need to supply the container in the function call in the init() function:

```
function init() {
    doHeadings('div#headings');
    doMenu();
    doForm();
}
```

We'll look out for any other opportunities to generalize the code.

Iterating Through the Headings Collection

The data you get from querySelectorAll() is called a **Node List**. It's not actually an array, but it is similar to an array in that it is a numbered collection. It's also similar in that you can iterate through the collection with the forEach() method.

The forEach() method takes as a parameter a function that will do the actual work:

```
function doSomething(item, index, collection) {

}
```

```
headings.forEach(doSomething);
```

where item is each item in the collection, index is the number of each item, and collection is the whole collection for good measure. Most of the time we're only interested in the item.

The function doesn't have to be a permanent named function if you're only using it in the forEach() method. A function expression will do:

```
headings.forEach(function(item, index, collection) {

});
```

Modern JavaScript has a shorter syntax for function expressions:

```
headings.forEach((item, index, collection) => {

});
```

In our case, we will need to refer to each item of the collection (each heading), but not the rest of the parameters, so we can use a *shorter* syntax without the parentheses:

```
headings.forEach(item => {

});
```

In our doHeadings() function, we can use it as follows:

```
function doHeadings() {
    let headings = document.querySelectorAll('div#headings>h2');
    if(!headings.length) return;
```

```
headings.forEach(heading => {

});
}
```

The next step will be to make the headings do something.

Attaching the Toggle Behavior

The code to show and hide content will be in the form of a function called
`toggle()`. What we need to do here is to trigger the function when clicking
on the heading. We'll do that by assigning a `toggle()` function to the
`onclick` event property of each heading:

```
function doHeadings(container) {
    ...

    headings.forEach(heading => {
        heading.onclick = toggle;
    });
    function toggle() {

    }
}
```

Note that the function is defined *after* you assign it, which seems
backward. You can define the function before, of course, but this way may
be easier to follow.

JavaScript doesn't normally run out of sequence. However, the
JavaScript interpreter runs in more than one stage, and you'll find that it
processes all `var` and `function` statements before it actually runs the code.
We say that `var` and `function` statements are **hoisted** (moved up).

The newer `let` and `const` statements are *not* hoisted.

Changing the Appearance

At this point, we need to know a little about how CSS can show and hide things. A very simple example would be something like this:

```
div#headings>h2+div {
    display: none;
}
div#headings>h2.open+div {
    display: block;
}
```

The select div#headings>h2+div means a div that comes after an h2 element that is inside the div whose id is headings. Sometimes, you need to read the selector backward to get its sense in English. Here, the div is hidden by default since its display property is set to none.

If you assign a class of open to the h2, then the selector h2.open applies. In this case, it will become visible, as its display property has been set to block.

The preceding CSS will do the job, but you can make showing and hiding more interesting if you introduce a little (subtle) animation. The actual CSS in the project is

```
div#headings>h2+div {
    overflow: hidden;
    max-height: 0;
    opacity: 0;
    transition: max-height 250ms, opacity 1500ms;
}

div#headings>h2.open+div {
    max-height: 30em;
    opacity: 1;
}
```

257

Instead of abruptly hiding and showing the div with the display property, the max-height of the div is first set to 0. To avoid content spilling over, the overflow property is also set to hidden.

While we're at it, we set its opacity to 0 to make it invisible. This will allow us to fade it in later.

To show the div, we set its height to something large enough and set its opacity to 1. What makes the change more interesting is the transition property that says which properties should take their time and how long.

The hardest part is working out a reasonable value for the max-height property. If you set it too high, you'll be waiting too long before you see the content closing in. If you set it too low, it won't fit the content.

You will appreciate how much is actually being done in a few lines of CSS. All that is required of JavaScript is to toggle the class.

Toggling the Class

From JavaScript's perspective, the task is simple. When you click on the heading, you should add or remove the open class. The CSS will do the rest.

To toggle the class of the clicked heading, use the classList.toggle function:

```
function toggle(event) {
    event.target.classList.toggle('open');
}
```

Remember, event.target is the heading you just clicked on. The toggle function will look for the class open. If it finds it, the class will be removed. Otherwise, it will be added.

If you test this now, you will find that you can open and close any section by clicking on its heading. You will also see some animation that was written into the CSS for that class.

Selecting a Single Heading

As the code stands, you can open as many sections as you like. This behavior is similar to check boxes on a form where you can also select as many as you like. You might prefer to have only one section open at a time, similar to selecting one of many radio buttons on a form.

Selecting one section at a time will require more work, as you will also need to track which section is already open so that you can close it while opening the new one.

First, we'll need another variable, say, opened, to remember the currently open section:

```
function doHeadings() {
    ...

    let opened = null;
    function toggle(event) {
        // event.target.classList.toggle('open');
    }
}
```

The opened variable will be used to track the h2 element that currently has the class open. To begin with, no section is open, so the variable opened is initialized with null.

Note that the original statement inside the toggle function has been commented out. What follows will be a replacement for that code. You can, of course, delete that statement, but it's kept here for comparison.

Note also how the new variable relates to the inner and outer functions. The opened variable is defined inside the doHeadings function, so it is *local* to doHeadings. However, it is defined outside the outer toggle function. There is no official term for this, but we can informally refer to this as **relatively global**.

The closest you'll get to a correct name for a relatively global variable is something like a **closure variable**. A **closure** is a function combined with its inherited environment, in this case the variable.

You can learn more about closures at `https://developer.mozilla.org/en-US/docs/Web/JavaScript/Closures`.

The first job of the `toggle` function should be to hide the previous section; that is to remove the open class from the currently selected h2:

```
function toggle(event) {
    //  event.target.classList.toggle('open');
    opened.classList.remove('open');    //  not yet
}
```

The `classList.remove` function will look for the open class in the element and remove it if it's there; it has no effect if it isn't.

If you try this, you'll get an error to begin with. That's because no section is open, and opened is set to null; you can't call methods on `null`. This means we'll have to test it first:

```
function toggle(event) {
    //  event.target.classList.toggle('open');
    if(opened) opened.classList.remove('open');
}
```

Remember that `if( ... )` will test for `true` or `false`, but also for something or nothing. In this case, `null` counts as nothing; if opened is something, we can remove the class.

The next step will be to open the selected section by adding open to the selected h2's class list. We will also assign that h2 as the new opened variable:

```
function toggle(event) {
    //  event.target.classList.toggle('open');
    if(opened) opened.classList.remove('open'); // close
    event.target.classList.add('open');
    opened = event.target;
}
```

If you run this now, you will see that only one section is opened
at a time.

Closing the Selected Section

The normal behavior of radio buttons is that once one is selected, one is
always selected. (You can see this in the radio button section at the bottom
of the page.) That's not always convenient for radio buttons, and neither is
it for opening sections. With a little more work, we can close the currently
open section when clicking on it again.

After closing the current section, you need to check whether the
selected heading is the same as last time. If it is, leave it closed and forget
it; if not, open it as before:

```
function toggle(event) {
    //  event.target.classList.toggle('open');

    if(opened) opened.classList.remove('open'); // close

    if(event.target == opened) {              // Forget
        opened = null;
    }
    else {                                    // Open & Remember
        event.target.classList.add('open');
        opened = event.target;
    }
}
```

Moving the doHeadings Code to the Library

Most of the code is fairly independent of the application, so we can move
it to the library for future use. We should probably think of a better name,
though. doHeadings is a little too vague.

If you can think of a better name than toggleHeadingContent, you're
welcome to go for it. For now, we'll assume that you can't.

First, you can move the whole of the doHeadings() function code
to the library.js file. There's already a reference to the library in the
showing-hiding.html page, so that's one less thing you have to worry
about. Don't forget to rename it.

There should be a comment block before the function. It should also
include some simple instructions, something like this:

```
/*  toggleHeadingContent(container)
    ==================================================
    Toggles heading sections. Use the following structure:

    div#containerid
        h2
        div
            content
        h2
        div
            content
        h2
        div         `
            content
    ================================================== */

    function toggleHeadingContent(container) {
        ...
    }
```

You can be as detailed as you like, but try not to get carried away.

Finally, of course, you'll need to change the name in the init() function code:

```
function init() {
    toggleHeadingContent('div#headings');
    doMenu();
    doForm();
}
```

We can now work on the code to toggle nested lists.

Toggling Lists

An HTML list is a structure that contains one or more list items. In its simplest form, the HTML looks like this:

```
<ul>
    <li>Apple</li>
    <li>Banana</li>
    <li>Cherry</li>
</ul>
```

which in the browser looks like this:

- Apple

- Banana

- Cherry

This particular list is called an **unordered list** and is marked up as ul; in principle, there is no significance in the item order. You can also have an **ordered list** marked up as ol, in which case item numbers are supplied automatically.

Using CSS, you can make many changes to the appearance of the list, including the numbering style.

You can also have **nested lists**, lists within lists:

```
<ul>
    <li>Fruit
        <ul>
            <li>apple</li>
            <li>banana</li>
            <li>cherry</li>
        </ul>
    </li>
    <li>Instruments
        <ul>
            <li>accordion</li>
            <li>banjo</li>
            <li>cor anglais</li>
        </ul>
    </li>
</ul>
```

which looks like this:

- Fruit
    - apple
    - banana
    - cherry
- Instruments
    - accordion
    - banjo
    - cor anglais

Here, the main list items have some text followed by another ul; the text acts as a heading for the nested list.

Lists are often used as a menu, ranging from simple navigation buttons to menus with drop-down submenus, all through the magic of CSS.

If the list is large enough, it starts to dominate the page, and it becomes convenient to find a way of opening and closing sections of the list. This is what we're working on in this part of the project.

Lists can, of course, be used for many things, but one common use is as lists of links to act as a menu. In the past, other structures, such as tables, were also used for menus due to the difficulty of making them look right, especially if the menu was supposed to be horizontal.

Thankfully, those days are over, and CSS can make list menus look just right. The hardest part now is deciding which of the many ways you want to style your lists.

The Initial JavaScript

The main list is in an unordered list as follows:

```
<ul id="menu>

</ul>
```

The CSS has made a number of changes to its appearance, including the fact that nested lists are hidden:

```
ul#menu li>ul { /*  ul inside li inside ul#menu */
    display: none;
}
```

As with the headings shown previously, we want the code to be reusable, so we'll include a parameter in the doMenu() function and use it in the init() function:

```
function init() {
    toggleHeadingContent('div#headings');
    doMenu('menu');
}

function doMenu(menuId) {

}
```

Here, we're simply passing an id, assuming that it must be the id of a ul element.

Inside the doMenu() function, we can use the id to locate the list:

```
function doMenu(menuId) {
    let ul = document.querySelector(`ul#${menuId}`);
}
```

Unlike the aforementioned headings, we won't need to attach the event listener to individual elements inside the list. This is because if you click on an element inside, that click is **propagated** to its container, so the one event listener will be able to handle it.

To attach the event listener, assign the onclick property as usual:

```
function doMenu() {
    let ul = document.querySelector('ul#menu');
    ul.onclick = toggle;

    function toggle(event) {

    }
}
```

Remember that an event listener added using the `onclick` event property defaults to listening in the bubble phase, that is, from the inside out. That's exactly what we want.

The `ul` variable is used only once, so we might dispense with it with the statement:

```
// Not this time:
document.querySelector('ul#menu').onclick = toggle;
```

However, we will need the `ul` variable to make a further improvement later, so we'll leave it in the original form.

Now, the list is a large structure with many other list items and lists inside. The event listener will respond to a click on any of these nested elements. What you need to know is what element you actually clicked on so that we can change its state.

Event listeners have access to *two* values that relate to the event:

- The `event.target` variable refers to the element that has the event listener attached. In this case, it is always the `ul#menu` element.

- The `event.currentTarget` property refers to the element that triggered the event listener; that is the one you actually clicked on.

In many of our previous examples, the element you clicked on was the same as the one with the event listener, so `event.currentTarget` and `event.target` refer to the same thing. This time they will be different, and you need to distinguish between. This time we refer to the event listener as the **delegated** event listener.

The next thing we need to worry about is whether there is a nested list to show. The `event.target` is always an `li` element, since that is the visible part of the list on the page. *Some* of these items will have a nested list, and some won't.

We can test for a nested list using `event.target.`
`querySelector('ul')`:

```
function toggle(event) {
    if(!event.target.querySelector('ul')) return;
}
```

We limit the querySelector to this one `li` element. The result of `event.target.querySelector('ul')` is either something (another list) or nothing (`null`). If it's not something (`if(!...)`), we exit the function with the `return` statement. Otherwise, we go on to toggle the item:

```
function toggle(event) {
    if(!event.target.querySelector('ul')) return;
    event.target.classList.toggle('open');
}
```

You can now open and close nested lists.

Highlighting Nested Lists

Of course, not all list items have nested lists. Ideally you would highlight those which do. In this case, they are highlighted with the › character, which is rotated when the item is open.

Traditionally, CSS had no selector that will select an element that has particular contents, so you would have to use a brute force approach in JavaScript.

Modern CSS does have such a selector. However, it's brand new and not yet properly supported in Firefox. The selector takes the following form:

```
li:has(ul) {
    ...
}
```

which means any `li` that contains a `ul`. If you look at the style sheet itself, it's not quite so simple, since it still has to cater for nonsupporting browsers:

```
li:is(.nested,:has(ul)) {
    ...
}
```

There's more to the selectors since they include references to the `open` class, the `ul#menu` main list, and other content.

The point is nonsupporting browsers will need some help in the form of a class, called `nested`.

Supporting Nonsupporting Browsers

Currently, most, but not all, browsers support the `:has()` selector, quite possibly yours included. However, you should always allow for nonsupport for *newer* features.

You can get some idea of how well supported a newer feature by visiting `https://caniuse.com/`.

To get this working cross-platform, then, we'll need to add the `nested` class to the items with nested lists on nonsupporting browsers. We don't want to do this manually, so we'll get JavaScript to do the hard work.

In the past, there was an awful lot of "browser sniffing" – checking which browser was being used. That's definitely a bad idea, since it was impossible to keep up with the various browsers and versions. A far better idea is testing for the feature itself.

You should only consider this sort of thing if the feature has been standardized but not yet completely supported across the board. Relying on nonstandard features will guarantee heartache in the future.

In the past, many of the JavaScript features we have used in this book, such as `.forEach()`, or `.querySelector()` or `.classList`, required testing. That's why there are so many references to "Modern JavaScript." Fortunately, they've all been supported for many years, as a look at `https://caniuse.com/` will confirm.

To test for a new CSS feature, there is a function called `CSS.supports()` that will test whether a particular CSS feature is available. What we're looking for is something like this:

```
CSS.supports('selector(:has(ul))')
```

The `selector()` function inside the string tests whether a particular selector will work; the selector `:has(ul)` is the specific pseudoclass selector we want. If the feature is supported, the result will be true; otherwise, it will be `false`.

We'll use this to add the `nested` class to these list items, but only if we need to. Previously, we found the main list and assigned it to the variable `ul`. Using this, we can search its contents:

```
function doMenu() {
    let ul=document.querySelector('ul#menu');
    ul.onclick=toggle;

    if(!CSS.supports('selector(:has(ul))')) {
        ul.querySelectorAll('li').forEach(li => {
```

```
    });
  }
  ...
}
```

The ul.querySelectorAll('li') will generate a collection of list items inside the ul list. As we have seen before, you can iterate through this collection using .forEach(). Note that the items discovered will be *all* of the list items, including those further inside nested lists and those without their own nested list.

Inside the forEach, we have an arrow function, assigning each list item to the variable li. Here, we will want to select only those list items that themselves contain a list:

```
function doMenu() {
    let ul=document.querySelector('ul#menu');
    ul.onclick=toggle;

    if(!CSS.supports('selector(:has(ul))')) {
        ul.querySelectorAll('li').forEach(li => {
            if(li.querySelector('ul')) li.classList.
            add('nested');
        });
    }
    ...
}
```

The li.querySelector('ul') looks for a ul element inside each li. If it finds one, we don't want the actual element, but we want to add the nested class to the li. If it fails to find one, the result is null, and the rest will be ignored.

There's some discussion in bug reports about whether CSS.supports('selector(:has(ul))') will test correctly. In the author's experience, it works well. If you have your doubts, you can forget about testing the feature and add the class anyway:

```
function doMenu() {
    let ul=document.querySelector('ul#menu');
    ul.onclick=toggle;
//  if(!CSS.supports('selector(:has(ul))')) {
        ul.querySelectorAll('li').forEach(li => {
            if(li.querySelector('ul')) li.classList.
            add('nested');
        });
//  }
    ...
}
```

It doesn't hurt to have both.

Fixing the toggle() Function

In the toggle() function, we included a test for whether the list item includes a nested list:

```
if(!event.target.querySelector('ul')) return;
```

Repeatedly looking through the DOM is a little expensive, so we can take advantage of the fact that we already know whether there is a nested list: either the :has(ul) applies or it has the nested class (or both). We can test for either using the .matches() method, which tests where a CSS selector applies:

```
function toggle(event) {
    if(!event.target.matches(':is(.nested,:has(ul))')) return;
    event.target.classList.toggle('open');
}
```

The `.matches()` method tests whether an element would match a CSS selector. For example:

```
»   var h1 = document.querySelector('h1');
»   h1.matches('body *');
←   true
```

This tells us that the h1 element is inside the body element, which, of course, it is.

The `:is(.nested,:has(ul))` selector succeeds if either the `.nested` selector or `:has(ul)` selector matches. If not, we return from the function.

Testing for properties is more efficient than searching inside an element for more elements.

Moving the List Toggle to the Library

Again, the code was written so that it's not specific to the application. All that's required is that the list is nested and that we know the id.

We can move the code to the `lilbrary.js` file using a name such as `toggleNestedLists()`, or whatever you like. Again, we should add a helpful comment block before it, something like

```
/*  toggleNestedLists(menuId)
    =================================================
    Toggles nested lists.

    The structure should be something like:

    <ul id="...">
```

```
            <li>item
                <ul>
                    <li>item</li>
                    <li>item</li>
                </ul>
            </li>
            <li>item
                <ul>
                    <li>item</li>
                    <li>item</li>
                </ul>
            </li>
        </ul>

    ================================================== */

    function toggleNestedLists(menuId) {
        ...
    }
```

Don't forget to change the name of the function in your init()
function:

```
function init() {
    toggleHeadingContent('div#headings');
    toggleNestedLists('menu');
}
```

This is now ready to use in other projects.

Enhancing Radio Buttons

Earlier, we mentioned the behavior of radio buttons.

Radio buttons are a type of form element that allows the user to select one of a number of choices. When you select one, the others are deselected. The name comes from a period in ancient history when car radios had push buttons to select a radio station.

It was mentioned earlier that once you've selected a radio button, you can't deselect them all – there's always one selected. The user-friendly way to allow choosing none is to include a None of the above option.

Alternatively, using JavaScript, we can instill the same sort of behavior as with the headings in this chapter: selecting one that is already selected will deselect it.

At the bottom of the page is a simple form with some radio buttons, an output element, and a submit button.

The HTML is something like this:

```
<form id="music">
    <p>Choose a musical style</p>
    <label><input type="radio" name="musical-style"
        value="jazz">Jazz</label>
    <label><input type="radio" name="musical-style"
        value="classical">Classical</label>
    <label><input type="radio" name="musical-style"
        value="newage">New Age</label>
    <label><input type="radio" name="musical-style"
        value="rocknroll">Rock & Roll</label>
    <output name="selected">
    <button name="ok">OK</button>
</form>
```

Nobody's suggesting that it's a very useful form.

In HTML, a group of radio buttons has these two features:

- They are all of the radio type: `<input type="radio">`.

- They all have the same name attribute, which is how the browser knows they're part of the same group.

When the form is submitted, only the selected radio button is submitted. If none is selected, then nothing of that name will be submitted.

The first thing we'll do is find the form and disable submitting it:

```
function doForm() {
    let form = document.querySelector('form#music');

    form.elements['ok'].onclick = event => {
        event.preventDefault();
    };
}
```

The next thing is to get the radio buttons:

```
function doForm() {
    let form = document.querySelector('form#music');
    let buttons = form.elements['musical-style'];

    ...
}
```

Normally, when you fetch from the elements collection, you get a single form element. In the case of radio buttons, you get another collection; more specifically it's a **RadioNodeList**, but we're only interested in the fact that we can iterate through the collection.

Remember in the contents headings, we wanted to select one element only. That behavior is built in to radio buttons. However, we also wanted to be able to deselect a heading, and that certainly isn't built in to radio buttons. We'll use the same technique of using a tracking variable.

We'll declare a variable to track the currently selected button:

```
function doForm() {
    let form = document.querySelector('form#music');
    let buttons = form.elements['musical-style'];
    let selected = null;

    ...

}
```

We'll now attach an event listener to each of the radio buttons to maintain this tracking variable:

```
function doForm() {
    let form = document.querySelector('form#music');
    let buttons = form.elements['musical-style'];
    let selected = null;

    buttons.forEach(b => {
        b.onclick = event => {

        };
    });

    ...

}
```

We've got two arrow function expressions here: one to iterate through the buttons collection and one for the event listener.

The event listener will check whether the clicked button is the same as last time. If it is, we'll deselect the button by setting its .checked property to false and clearing out the selected variable.

If it's not the same, we'll just remember that in the selected variable.

The first time, of course, there was no last time, so the answer will be false.

```
buttons.forEach(b => {
    b.onclick = event => {
        if(event.target == selected) {
            event.target.checked = false;
            selected = null;
        }
        else selected = event.target;
    };
});
```

Reusing the Deselectable Radio Button Code

As always, if the code is useful, we may be able to wrap it into a reusable function.

The first step is to create a new function. We'll call it deselectableRadio(). We can then move the main part of the code into it:

```
function doForm() {

}

function deselectableRadio(buttons) {
    buttons.forEach(b => {
        b.onclick = event => {
            if(event.target == selected) {
                event.target.checked = false;
                selected = null;
            }
            else selected = event.target;
        };
    });
}
```

The function will receive the buttons collection.

To avoid having to maintain a separate variable, we can turn that into a function property:

```
function deselectableRadio(buttons) {
    deselectableRadio.selected ??= null;
    buttons.forEach(b => {
        b.onclick = event => {
            if(event.target == deselectableRadio.selected) {
                event.target.checked = false;
                deselectableRadio.selected = null;
            }
            else deselectableRadio.selected = event.target;
        };
    });
}
```

We should now be able to test the function. Comment out the old code, just in case, and include a call to the new function, passing the buttons collection:

```
function doForm() {
    let form = document.querySelector('form#music');
    let buttons = form.elements['musical-style'];
    deselectableRadio(buttons);
/*
    ...
*/
    form.elements['ok'].onclick = event => {
        event.preventDefault();
    };
}
```

```
function deselectableRadio(buttons) {
    ...
}
```

If it works, you can delete the commented code and move the function to `library.js` as you did with the other functions in this chapter. You can include a comment block like this:

```
/*  deselectableRadio(buttons)
    =================================================
    Allows a group of radio buttons to be deselected.
    ================================================= */
```

Of course, you may not want your radio buttons to be deselectable, but it's nice to have a choice.

Summary

In this project, we used JavaScript to show and hide content with user interaction. We used many of the concepts developed in Chapter 7.

You can show and hide content in CSS. One simple method is to change the `display` property between `block` and `none`, which is the method used in the nested list. A more complex method, which allows transition animation effects, is to change the `max-height` and `opacity` properties.

The main thrust of the code is to use the `click` event to toggle the class of the element. The CSS handles what happens to the content that is either nested or adjacent to the affected element.

In the headings exercise, there are multiple elements that need to be attached to the event listener. These are fetched using the `.querySelectorAll()` function. We can then iterate through the collection with the `.forEach()` method.

In the nested list exercise, we attached a single delegate event listener to the main list and let the event bubble from the selected list item. We then use `event.target` to toggle the specific element.

A simple toggle would allow multiple elements to be in the same state, like check boxes on a form. By managing the selected element with a separate variable, it's possible to select only one at a time, like radio buttons on a form. It's also possible to deselect all of them.

Modern CSS includes a selector for elements that contain other elements. This should simplify writing code for list items that have nested lists, but this feature is not yet fully supported by all browsers. However, it's possible to test for this feature in JavaScript, search for these particular elements, and assign a class that substitutes for this feature.

Finally, we wrote some code that modified the behavior of radio buttons to allow deselecting all of the buttons.

When the code is complete, we can move the code to the library file, as long as it's not specific to our current project.

Coming Up

The content we've been working with is already there in the page – it's just being hidden. In Chapter 10, we'll look at how to load new content on demand.

Before that, however, we're going to work on a lightbox project. This is where images pop up on the screen on demand. To do this, we'll work through adding HTML content, adding CSS, and triggering activity with the mouse and the keyboard.

In Chapter 10, we'll also work on loading image content and data from the server using Ajax.

Project: Building a Lightbox Gallery

Many modern image gallery pages include a pop-up larger image. This has come to be known as **lightbox** after an original script by Lokesh Dhakar (see `https://en.wikipedia.org/wiki/Lightbox_(JavaScript)`).

You will have seen something similar on many websites. When you click on an image thumbnail, a larger one appears over the rest of the page. A typical lightbox effect looks like Figure 9-1.

© Mark Simon 2023
M. Simon, *JavaScript for Web Developers*, https://doi.org/10.1007/978-1-4842-9774-2_9

Figure 9-1. *A lightbox gallery*

You can see a sample lightbox gallery in action at `https://pure-javascript.net/lightbox.html`.

In this project, you will write your own JavaScript lightbox function that you can use on many other projects. Apart from the usefulness of having your own JavaScript widget, you will learn more about

- Hijacking HTML anchors

- Creating a reusable and adaptable JavaScript widget

- Creating HTML elements and CSS styles in JavaScript

- Creating a pop-up element

- Triggering CSS changes with JavaScript events

- Dealing with asynchronous image loading

- Responding to keyboard events

An important part of the lightbox is its visual appearance, which is controlled by CSS, including some animation. You'll learn how to generate enough essential CSS to make the widget work, while at the same time allowing a designer to override some of the appearance.

At the end of this chapter, we'll also revisit the slide show from Chapter 4. By then, we'll have developed additional skills in working with dynamic CSS, and we'll add a few more features to make the slide show a little more interesting to look at.

Preparing the HTML

The JavaScript code should be as unobtrusive as you can make it, so you shouldn't need much in the way of additional preparation.

In this case, we want the HTML to be as natural as possible. If you open the file lightbox.html in your editor and look at the code, you will see a collection of linked images inside a main container:

```
<div id="catalogue">
    <a href="..."><img src="..." title="..."></a>
    <a href="..."><img src="..." title="..."></a>
    <a href="..."><img src="..." title="..."></a>
    <!-- etc -->
<div>
```

In this case, the container is a div element, which is the most generic block element. We can use the id catalogue to identify the container to be processed. The id is also used in CSS to give the container and contents any special appearance you like.

The images will be ordinary img elements showing thumbnail versions in the src attribute. We have omitted other attributes here, but the title attribute is useful. Normally, the title appears as tooltip text when you hover the mouse over it, but we will use it as caption text for the larger image.

Each image is wrapped inside an anchor (a) element linking to a larger version of the image. By itself, the anchor would normally reload the page with the linked image, but we'll use it to display the larger image in a popup instead.

The Initial HTML and JavaScript

As with the previous project, we will create a separate flexible function that can easily be relocated to the library file. For now, we'll keep it in the main JavaScript file for simplicity.

The HTML file is called lightbox.html, and the corresponding JavaScript file is lightbox.js.

The HTML already includes the references to the JavaScript files:

```
<script type="text/javascript" src="scripts/library.js"
    crossorigin="anonymous"></script>
<script type="text/javascript" src="scripts/lightbox.js"
    crossorigin="anonymous" defer></script>
```

The JavaScript starts in the usual way, but we have already included a call to the new function complete with a parameter for the container of the images:

```
init();
function init() {
    doLightbox('div#catalogue');
}

function doLightbox(container) {

}
```

If you load the page now and click on one of the images, all you'll see is that the page is reloaded with the larger image. That's because the larger image is referenced in the href attribute of the surrounding anchor.

You'll also see that the color of each of the thumbnails is desaturated (mostly grayscale) when the mouse isn't over it. That's all done in CSS.

Inside the doLightbox() function, we can use the selector string with querySelectorAll() to find the anchors containing the images:

```
function doLightbox(container) {
    let anchors = document.querySelectorAll(`${container}>a`);
}
```

As you'll recall, the template literal `${container}>a` allows you to include expressions and variables inside. In the preceding code, the selector string translates to

```
let anchors = document.querySelectorAll('div#catalogue>a');
```

which means all of the anchors that are children of the div element.

Once we have these anchors, we can change their behavior to load the larger image into a popup.

Hijacking the Anchors

Normally, an anchor is used to link to a new document or page. Here, we will use it to display a larger image instead. That means we need to change from the default behavior to a new behavior. This is often referred to as **hijacking** the anchor.

To add our own behavior, we will need to add an event listener on the click event to all of the anchors:

```
function doLightbox(container) {
    let anchors = document.querySelectorAll(`${container}>a`);
    anchors.forEach(a => {
        a.onclick = show;
    });

    //  Showing & Hiding
        function show(event) {

        }
}
```

The forEach() function iterates through each of the members of the anchors collection. The arrow function expression a => {} temporarily assigns each anchor to the variable a, so we can set its onclick event listener to the show function.

The show function will be using the event parameter.

We need to solve a logistic problem with anchors. Even though we have diverted the click to our function, the normal behavior of an anchor would still have loaded the browser with new content, which would be the larger image in the href attribute; this new content *replaces* the old content.

Instead, we will display the new content on the current page, so we need to cancel the normal behavior. This is done with the preventDefault() function:

```
function show(event) {
    event.preventDefault();
}
```

The preventDefault() function can be used whenever an HTML element has a dynamic behavior, such as a button in a form or an anchor as before. You can call the preventDefault() function any time in the show function, but it's often called at the beginning.

We'll also need the event object again to get the details of the images.

If you reload the page, it won't do much. In fact, it won't do anything. Clicking on an image no longer loads the larger image, because we've intercepted that.

We'll write the code to show the image later. First, we need to create somewhere to put the image.

Creating the Pop-Up Elements

To display the larger image as a popup, you will need some extra HTML and CSS. You could have created this in the original documents, but it's better if JavaScript does this for you. This way, there are no additional requirements of the document.

This is an important principle when writing JavaScript utilities of this nature. The HTML elements and CSS required to implement the lightbox are additional to the original content of the page. It's appropriate to leave the original content alone and let JavaScript manage the additional content.

We'll need four additional HTML elements for the popup:

- There will be a background div that will cover the whole screen.

  The background will serve two purposes. First, it will mask the rest of the document by having a translucent background color. Second, you will be able to click on it to hide the background and the popup.

- There will be a container figure to contain the larger image and a caption.

- There is the pop-up image itself, which will be an img element.

- Finally, the caption will be in a figcaption element.

The pop-up elements will look something like Figure 9-2.

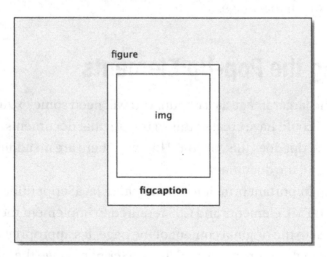

Figure 9-2. *The lightbox elements*

The figure, together with img and figcaption elements, will sit in front of the background div.

Creating the Elements

To create the elements, we use document.createElement():

```
function doLightbox(container) {
    let anchors = document.querySelectorAll(`${conainer}>a`);
    anchors.forEach(a => {
        a.onclick = show;
    });

    //  Create Elements
        let background = document.createElement('div');

        let figure = document.createElement('figure');
        let img = document.createElement('img');
        let figcaption = document.createElement('figcaption');

    ...
}
```

This should be enough for JavaScript to work with, but there's going to be a little CSS involved. To make sure that CSS doesn't get things mixed up, we'll add ids to the background and figure elements. The CSS will know how to handle the nested img and figcaption elements.

```
function (container) {
    ...

    //  Create Elements
        let background = document.createElement('div');
```

```
    let figure = document.createElement('figure');
    let img = document.createElement('img');
    let figcaption = document.createElement('figcaption');

    background.id = 'lightbox-background';
    figure.id = 'lightbox';

    ...
}
```

The background div will stand alone, but the image and caption should be contained inside the container element. This can be done using appendChild():

```
function doLightbox(container) {
    ...

    // Create Elements
    ...

    background.id = 'lightbox-background';
    figure.id = 'lightbox';

    figure.appendChild(img);
    figure.appendChild(figcaption);

    ...
}
```

The appendChild() function adds an element inside at the end of the content. This is a simpler version of insertAdjacentElement ('beforeend', ...).

Adding the Elements to the Document

At this point, the newly created elements are still floating around in memory. We'll add them to the document body the same way:

```
function (container) {
    ...

    // Create Elements
    ...
    figure.appendChild(img);
    figure.appendChild(figcaption);

    document.body.appendChild(background);
    document.body.appendChild(figure);

    ...
}
```

We now have some empty elements added to the end of the document body. If you reload the page, you won't see very much: all of the new elements are at the end of the body element, but they are empty, so they take up no space.

The next step will begin to define their appearance.

Styling the Additional Elements

You could add the CSS directly into the style sheet, but, as before, that means the developer needs to do extra work. It would be better if the styles were added by JavaScript.

In Chapter 7, on manipulating CSS, we created a style block in JavaScript. Here, we'll put the idea into practice.

To add the CSS style, you first create a `style` element and add it to the head of the document:

```
function doLightbox(container) {
    ...

    //  Create Elements
        ...

    //  Style Sheet
        let style = document.createElement('style');
        document.head.insertAdjacentElement('afterbegin',
        style);

    ...
}
```

Note that the new style element is added to the *beginning* of the head element. This allows additional real style sheets to be added after, meaning that they can override some of your own styles.

Adding Style Rules

Next, we will need to create some essential CSS rules to get the job done. Here is what the essential CSS would look like if you were to do this in a normal style sheet:

```
/*  Background Div: */
    div#lightbox-background {
        position: fixed;
        top: 0; left: 0; width:100%; height: 100%;
        z-index: 1;
        background-color: rgb(0,0,0,0.5);
    }
```

```
/*  Container Div: */
    figure#lightbox {
        position: fixed;
        top: 50%; left: 50%; margin-right: -50%;
        transform: translate(-50%, -50%);
        z-index: 2;
    }
```

The CSS works as follows:

- The background div needs to fill the whole screen,
  which is achieved by fixing its position relative to that
  of the screen (position: fixed) and setting its top left
  corner and dimensions.

- To achieve the effect of masking the rest of the screen,
  the background has a color of black (0,0,0), but an
  opacity setting of 0.5, which makes it translucent
  (partially see-through). It also has a nonzero z-index,
  which puts it in front of the other elements.

- The figure element is to be centered on the screen,
  which also requires fixing its position relative to the
  screen (position: fixed), but shifting its starting
  position half way.

- In order to ensure that the figure element appears
  in front of the background, its z-index property is set
  higher than that of the background.

The actual color and opacity of the background are arbitrary, and you
can easily override these values in an additional real style sheet.

The two sections in the CSS shown previously are called **rules** and can be added using insertRule():

```
function doLightbox(container) {
    ...

    //  Style Sheet
        let style = document.createElement('style');
        document.head.insertAdjacentElement('afterbegin',
        style);

    //  Lightbox Element Styles
        style.sheet.insertRule(`
            div#lightbox-background {
                position: fixed;
                top: 0; left: 0; width:100%; height: 100%;
                z-index: 1;
                background-color: rgb(0,0,0,0.5);
            }
        `);
        style.sheet.insertRule(`
            figure#lightbox {
                position: fixed;
                top: 50%; left: 50%; margin-right: -50%;
                transform: translate(-50%, -50%);
                z-index: 2;
            }
        `);

    ...
}
```

We've used template literals to allow line breaks and indentation also for readability. Remember, CSS can have as much additional spacing as you like.

As you see, CSS has a tendency to get verbose, so it will never be very compact. Fortunately, that's enough CSS to achieve the effect.

What you'll see now is the whole page covered by the translucent background. The figure appears as a small box but is otherwise invisible because it has no content yet.

Hiding and Showing the Elements

The whole trick to the lightbox is that the background and container will appear only when you select an image and will disappear when you've finished looking at it.

Showing and Hiding the Background

You've started writing the show() function to show the image, and now you can add a hide() function to hide it:

```
function doLightbox(container) {
    ...

    // Showing & Hiding

        function show(event) {
            event.preventDefault();
        }
        function hide(event) {

        }
}
```

To hide an element, you can set its `display` property to `none`. To show the element, set its `display` property to `block`, how we normally want them displayed:

```
function doLightbox(container) {

    ...

    // Showing & Hiding

        function show(event) {
            event.preventDefault();

            background.style.display
                = figure.style.display
                = 'block';
        }
        function hide(event) {
            background.style.display
                = figure.style.display
                = 'none';
        }
}
```

The preceding code uses chained assignment statements to set more than one property. The main reason for this is to make clear that you're setting the two properties to the same value.

You don't need to show or hide the image or caption elements, since they are part of the container element.

You have already attached the `show()` function to the `click` event of the anchors. To hide everything, you can attach the `hide()` function to the `click` event of the background:

```
function doLightbox(container) {

    ...
```

```
//  Showing & Hiding
  background.onclick = hide;

  function show(event) {
    ...
  }
  ...
}
```

This effectively turns the background into one giant button. You can click on the background now to hide it, but you should also call the hide() function when the script is first loaded:

```
function doLightbox(container) {
  ...

  //  Showing & Hiding
    background.onclick=hide;
    hide(); //  hide now

    ...
}
```

At this stage, you can test showing and hiding by clicking on an image and the background, but all you'll see is the background showing and hiding. Next, you'll need to populate the container with the image and its caption.

Showing the Image Content

The next part is to show the image and its caption. This basically means showing the figure, but first you will need to populate the image and caption paragraph.

Recall that the image is inside an anchor:

```
<a href="...">
    <img src="..." title="...">
</a>
```

The anchor itself is just a wrapper, and most of the visual space will be taken by the image. Therefore, when you click on this, you will actually be clicking on the image.

The image doesn't have an event listener and has no default clicking behavior, so it has no interest in the click. That click event is passed on to its container, the anchor element. As we saw in Chapter 7 on event listeners, the event has **bubbled**.

We can prevent bubbling from happening, but in this case, that's exactly what we want. The containing anchor *does* have an event listener, and it is this function that will do the job.

In summary, you click on the image, but the anchor will process the click.

Inside the event listener, there are two important objects:

- The event.target refers to the element you actually clicked on: the image.

- On the other hand, event.currentTarget is a reference to the element that has the event listener attached to it: the anchor.

We'll need both. The currentTarget, which is the anchor, has a reference to a larger element in its href property. The target, which is the image, has the text for the caption in its title attribute.

When we show the larger image, we want to copy the URL from the anchor's href into the pop-up image's src attribute. That means copying the href from currentTarget:

```
function show(event) {
    event.preventDefault();

    // populate image element
        img.src = event.currentTarget.href;

    background.style.display = figure.style.display = 'block';
}
```

As for the caption, that will come from the original image's title attribute. That means copying the title from the event.target to the caption's textContent:

```
function show(event) {
    event.preventDefault();

    // populate image element
        img.src = event.currentTarget.href;
    // caption text
        figcaption.textContent = event.target.title;

    background.style.display = container.style.display =
    'block';
}
```

The pop-up image element is currently devoid of the alt and title attributes. These properties are always a good idea for images. We can copy them at the same time:

```
function show(event) {
    event.preventDefault();

    // populate image element
        img.src = event.currentTarget.href;
    // caption text
```

```
    figcaption.textContent = img.alt = img.title
        = event.target.title;
```

```
    background.style.display=container.style.display='block';
}
```

You won't see the image's alt or title attributes, but the alt is required in case the image can't be seen, and the title will typically appear if you hover the mouse over the image.

If you load the page now, it will work, but it will show and hide very abruptly. Later, we'll make that more interesting.

First, however, we'll need to solve a little problem of timing.

Timing Problems

If you test the code on your own machine, you may find that things work mostly as intended. However, if you run the code from a real web server, there may be problems due to a delay in loading the image.

For example, if you change the href in the first anchor to

```
<a href="http://pure-javascript.net/images/random.jpg">...</a>
```

there will be a short delay when you click on it. However, this delay will be long enough that the image won't appear in the popup.

The problem is inherent in the way JavaScript runs. Here is a simple script to illustrate the problem:

```
»    var image = new Image();
»    image.src =
        `http://pure-javascript.net/images/random.jpg?${Math.
        random()}`;
»    console.log(image.width);
```

The `image` variable is a virtual image for testing purposes. You won't actually see the image. Adding the random query string after `random.jpg` ensures that the browser doesn't cache the image, since that would interfere with the experiment.

The statement `image.src = ...;` causes the browser to request an image from the server. However, that could take some time, and JavaScript doesn't like to hang around waiting. As a result, the next line `console.log(...)` will run *before* the new image has arrived, so `image.width` won't be ready. You will probably get 0, or possibly a previous value.

We say that the image is loaded **asynchronously**. That's also going to be a problem later when working with Ajax, which also involves communicating with the web server.

Modern JavaScript has new methods for dealing with asynchronous code, but the delay with images is easily handled with something more traditional. An image can have a `load` event listener, which will be triggered when the image has fully arrived. We can use that to delay running part of the code:

```
var image = new Image();
```

```
function doit(event) {
    console.log(image.width);
}
```

```
image.onload = doit;
```

```
image.src =
  `https://pure-javascript.net/images/random.jpg?${Math.random()}`;
```

```
console.log('Meanwhile ...');
```

Now the `console.log(...);` statement will wait for the image to be loaded, and the result will be correct.

Notice that the message Meanwhile will be printed *before* the image width, as it is executed without waiting.

This event listener is simple enough not to require a named function, so we can use a function expression:

```
»    image.onload = function(event) {
         console.log(image.width);
     }
```

or the simpler arrow function expression:

```
»    image.onload = event => {
         console.log(image.width);
     }
```

Back to our lightbox project, we can use this idea to hold off displaying the popup until the image has arrived:

```
function show(event) {
    event.preventDefault();

    //  populate image element
        img.src = event.currentTarget.href;
    //  caption text
        figcaption.textContent = img.alt = img.title
            = event.target.title;

    //  background.style.display = figure.style.
    display='block';
    img.onload = event => {
        background.style.display = figure.style.display =
        'block';
    };
}
```

Now we have prepared the content for displaying, but only display once the image has arrived.

You can now test the project.

Adding Keyboard Control

So far, the lightbox gallery is controlled using the mouse, and that's fine as far as it goes. You can also add some keyboard control to the gallery. At the very least, you should be able to cancel the popup with something like the Escape key, but we can also add some keys to navigate the gallery.

Here is the keyboard behavior we want to implement:

Key	Behavior
escape	Hide image
home or ↑	First image
←	Previous imageIf at the beginning, wrap around to the last image
→	Next imageIf at the end, wrap around to the first image
end or ↓	Last image

As with everything else, this will be done with event listeners.

Adding Keyboard Event Listeners

You can add a keyboard event listener to an individual element, such as a textarea element in a form, but here we have nothing to focus the keyboard on. In this case, we will add the event listener to the document itself.

So as not to interfere with normal use of the keyboard in the rest of the page, we will assign an event listener only when the image is shown and remove it when it is hidden. We'll call the function doKeys().

```
function show(event) {
    ...
    document.addEventListener('keydown',doKeys);
}
function hide(event) {
    ...
    document.removeEventListener('keydown',doKeys);
}

function doKeys(event) {

}
```

JavaScript has a number of ways to react to a keyboard event, including keydown, keyup, and keypress, which occur at different stages of pressing a key. They also differ in how they respond to the noncharacter keys such as the shift key. For our keys, the keydown event seems to work best.

The doKeys() event listener function starts off like any other event listener:

```
function doLightbox(container) {
    //  --snip--
    function doKeys(event) {
        event.preventDefault();

    }
}
```

Later we will allow the arrow keys to navigate through the image collection. However, they normally scroll the page around, so we want to stop that while the image is showing. Adding preventDefault() will prevent any such keystrokes from being further processed.

Checking the Pressed Key

We will need to check which key was pressed. This information is available in the event.key property. You may find some legacy code that uses a different property, which was problematic in the extreme, since different browsers had different values for the keys. Fortunately the more modern event.key property is simpler and more reliable.

Eventually, we will respond to a number of different keys, so it's easier to use a switch statement to choose between them.

A switch statement is like a specialized if ... else if ... else if ... else block. It's used to test an unknown against a number of alternative values.

For example, we can get a user's number and test it as follows (use shift-return between lines if you want to test it):

```
»    var n = prompt('Choose 1 ... 4');
     if(n==1) {
         console.log('one');
     }
     else if(n==2) {
         console.log('two');
     }
     else if(n==3) {
         console.log('three');
     }
```

```
else if(n==4) {
    console.log('four');
}
else {
    console.log('whatever');
}
```

The switch statement does *nearly* the same thing, but not quite. To begin with, it looks like this, but it won't work yet:

```
» var n = prompt('Choose 1 ... 4');
  switch(n) {
      case 1:
          console.log('one');
      case 2:
          console.log('two');
      case 3:
          console.log('three');
      case 4:
          console.log('four');
      default:
          console.log('whatever');
  }
```

In principle, you're matching the variable n against the various values. If it doesn't match anything, it falls through to the default case.

The first thing you'll notice is that entering a number won't match. For reasons unknown, the switch statement doesn't do JavaScript's normal automatic type conversion, and the string from the prompt() function doesn't match the numbers in the case blocks.

You can try with converting the value yourself:

```
»   var n = prompt('Choose 1 ... 4');
    switch(parseInt(n)) {

        ...

    }
```

Now you get to the next problem. If you enter, say, the number 2, you'll find that you get all of the output statements from two onward. Once you enter a case block, you continue through the rest of them, even if the following cases don't match. This is regarded as baffling even to experienced developers, but it's there for historical reasons. We'll even take advantage of that in a moment.

Meanwhile, the solution is to add a break statement to each case once we've dealt with it:

```
»   var n = prompt('Choose 1 ... 4');
    switch(parseInt(n)) {
        case 1:
            console.log('one');
            break;
        case 2:
            console.log('two');
            break;
        case 3:
            console.log('three');
            break;
        case 4:
            console.log('four');
            break;
        default:
            console.log('whatever');
    }
```

You don't add one after the `default` case because it's the last one and there's nowhere else to go.

Back to the project, we'll add the outline of the `switch` block to test for the various keys:

```
function doKeys(event) {
    event.preventDefault();

    switch(event.key) {

    }
}
```

Each key will be implemented in a different `case` block.

Hiding with the Escape Key

The first case will be to test for the Escape key and use it to hide the popup:

```
function doKeys(event) {
    event.preventDefault();

    switch(event.key) {
        case 'Esc': //  Old Version
        case 'Escape':
            hide();
            break;

    }
}
```

The correct value for the Escape key is `Escape`. However, some older browsers will use the older `Esc` name, so it's best to check for both. This is done by including an empty case with the alternative value and letting it fall through to the next case.

Note that we're taking advantage of the fact that the code continues through subsequent case blocks until either it encounters a break or it gets to the end. That's how we allow the Esc case to fall through to the Escape case.

You can now test the page and check that the Escape key does indeed hide the pop-up image.

Adding Navigation Keys

We will also use the arrow keys to navigate through the gallery. However, the code as it stands is only aware of the *current* image and has no way of showing the next or previous image.

To implement navigation, we will first need to **refactor** our code.

Refactoring the Image Load

Refactoring refers to changing the way the code is structured without changing its behavior. It's often done to improve the efficiency or reliability of the code, but in this case, it will be done to make it more flexible.

Currently, the larger image is loaded when you click on a gallery link, and the popup starts to appear. The information you need is available from the image you clicked on.

When it comes to navigating through the gallery, the popup has already appeared, and you will need to load new contents. This information is not directly available from the image you clicked on, so you will need a different approach:

- When you click on an image, the pop-up elements will appear as before.

- As a separate process, the pop-up image and title will be populated. This will allow you to navigate to other images independently of showing or hiding the popup.

There's another logistic problem related to using the keyboard. When you click on an image, the event's currentTarget and target are set to the anchor and nested image by the mouse's click event. However, when you press an arrow key, the new event's currentTarget and target are related to the keypress and are unrelated to any image.

First, we'll need to keep track of the image that is currently showing, since we will need to progress from there with the arrow keys. We can do this with a new variable:

```
function doLightbox(container) {
    let images = document.querySelectorAll(`${container}>a`);
    anchors.forEach(a => {
        a.onclick = show;
    });
    let currentAnchor;  //  current anchor
    ...
}
```

The currentAnchor variable will actually be a reference to the anchor that contains the image. It will be first set whenever you click on an image:

```
function doLightbox(container) {
    ...
    function show(event) {
        event.preventDefault();
        currentAnchor = event.currentTarget;
        ...
    }
    ...
}
```

We'll now change the reference to event.currentTarget to currentAnchor:

```
function show(event) {
    event.preventDefault();
    currentAnchor = event.currentTarget;
    //  populate image element
        img.src = currentAnchor.href;
    ...
}
```

The next step is to move the loading part of the code into a separate function. We'll call it loadImage():

```
function loadImage() {
    //  populate image element
        img.src = currentAnchor.href;
    //  caption text
    //  figcaption.textContent = img.alt = img.title
    //      = event.target.title;

    img.onload = event => {
        background.style.display = figure.style.display = 'block';
    };
}

function show(event) {
    event.preventDefault();
    currentAnchor = event.currentTarget;
    //  code moved to loadImage()
    document.addEventListener('keydown',doKeys);
}
```

We've also cut the code out of the show() function and temporarily replaced it with a comment.

Note that the `figcaption.textContent` = code is also commented out for the moment. That's because of the problem with the event targets: we no longer have a simple reference to the nested image element. However, it's easy to look inside the current anchor to get the reference using querySelector():

```
let currentImage = currentAnchor.querySelector('img');
```

We can then use the `currentImage` variable instead of the `event.target` property:

```
function loadImage() {
    let currentImage = currentAnchor.querySelector('img');
    //  populate image element
        img.src = currentAnchor.href;
    //  caption text
        figcaption.textContent = img.alt = img.title
            = currentImage.title;

    //  background.style.display = figure.style.
    display='block';
    img.onload = event => {
        background.style.display = figure.style.display =
        'block';
    };
}
```

Normally, we've been using `document.querySelector()`, which searches the whole document for a match. Here, we're limiting the search to the current anchor.

We can add that to our `loadImage()` function and use `currentImage` to extract the title.

Finally, instead of loading the image in the show function itself, we call the `loadImage()` function:

```
function show(event) {
    event.preventDefault();
    currentAnchor = event.currentTarget;
    loadImage();

    document.addEventListener('keydown',doKeys);
}
```

At this point, everything should work the same as before, but now we'll be able to reuse the loadImage() function from a different section of the code. That will be in response to the arrow keys.

Loading the Adjacent Image

We can now add the code to enable the arrow keys, as well as the home and end keys.

To begin with, we'll implement the left and right arrows. We can start by adding these to the switch:

```
switch(event.key) {
    case 'Esc': //  Old Version
    case 'Escape':
        hide();
        break;
    case 'Left':    // Old Version
    case 'ArrowLeft':
        //  previous image
        break;
    case 'Right':   // Old Version
    case 'ArrowRight':
        //  next image
        break;
}
```

In older browsers, the keys were called Left and Right but now have the word Arrow prepended. Again we do this with empty case blocks.

To get the previous or next anchor, you will need

- Previous anchor: currentAnchor.
  previousElementSibling

- Next anchor: currentAnchor.nextElementSibling

The previousElementSibling and nextElementSibling properties refer to the elements before or after the current element, skipping any white space or comments.

After that, you can call the loadImage() function and let it do the rest:

```
switch(event.key) {
    case 'Esc': //  Old Version
    case 'Escape':
        hide();
        break;
    case 'Left':    //  Old Version
    case 'ArrowLeft':
        currentAnchor = currentAnchor.previousElementSibling;
        loadImage();
        break;
    case 'Right':    //  Old Version
    case 'ArrowRight':
        currentAnchor = currentAnchor.nextElementSibling;
        loadImage();
        break;
}
```

If you test it, you will find an error if you try to go too far. There is no image before the first one and none after the last one. We'll need to take that into account, but first we'll work on selecting the first and last images.

Loading the First and Last Images

We can add two more switch blocks for the first and last images:

```
switch(event.key) {
    ...
    case 'Home':
    case 'Up':       // Old Version
    case 'ArrowUp':
        // first image
        break;
    case 'End':
    case 'Down':     // Old Version
    case 'ArrowDown':
        // last image
        break;
}
```

Again we have the old and new versions of the arrow key names; we also have home and end keys as synonyms for the up and down arrow keys, respectively.

JavaScript doesn't have a first or last sibling property, unlike adjacent siblings, so we will need a different approach.

Although it isn't possible to get the first or last siblings, it is possible to get the first or last children of an element. The trick is to find the parent of the current anchor and then get the first or last child of that parent. You can use something like this:

- First anchor: currentAnchor.parentNode. firstElementChild

- Last anchor: currentAnchor.parentNode. lastElementChild

The `parentNode` is the element that contains the current anchor: the container div. From there, you can select the first or last element, again skipping the white space and comments.

We can now add the code as follows:

```
switch(event.key) {
    ...
    case 'Home':
    case 'Up':       // Old Version
    case 'ArrowUp':
        currentAnchor = currentAnchor.parentNode.
        firstElementChild;
        loadImage();
        break;
    case 'End':
    case 'Down':    // Old Version
    case 'ArrowDown':
        currentAnchor = currentAnchor.parentNode.
        lastElementChild;
        loadImage();
        break;
}
```

Now, back to the problem of the left and right arrow keys. It would be reasonable to expect the collection to cycle; that is the image before the first should be the last in the collection, and the image after the last should be the first in the collection.

Wrapping Around the End

If you attempt to select before the first image or after the last one, you'll get an error to the effect that the currentAnchor variable is null. In JavaScript, you can use the **or** operator (||) to add an alternative. For example:

```
»    var a = null;
»    console.log(a || 'Banana');
     "Banana"
```

In the aforementioned, if the variable a had a real value, it would be used. In this case, it's a null, which is close enough to nothing, so the next value, Banana, is used. We say that the || expression is **short-circuited**.

With this information, we can use the first image if the next image is null, and likewise the last image if the previous image is null:

```
//   Previous Image
     currentAnchor = currentAnchor.previousElementSibling ||
         currentAnchor.parentNode.lastElementChild;
//   Next Image
     currentAnchor = currentAnchor.nextElementSibling ||
         currentAnchor.parentNode.firstElementChild;
```

You can now finish off the switch blocks:

```
switch(event.key) {
    ...
    case 'Left':    // Old Version
    case 'ArrowLeft':
        currentAnchor = currentAnchor.previousElementSibling ||
            currentAnchor.parentNode.lastElementChild;
        loadImage();
        break;
    case 'Right':    // Old Version
    case 'ArrowRight':
        currentAnchor = currentAnchor.nextElementSibling ||
            currentAnchor.parentNode.firstElementChild;
```

```
    loadImage();
    break;
...
}
```

You can now test the lightbox gallery complete with keyboard navigation.

Adding CSS Special Effects

If you test the live version, you will notice that the image shows with an animation (which may or may not be to your liking). This effect is purely in CSS, and the only involvement of JavaScript is to trigger it.

You don't really need the full details, but the important part is in the following CSS:

```
figure#lightbox {
    transform-origin: 0 0;
    transition:
        transform 1s cubic-bezier(0.175, 0.885, 0.32, 1.275),
        opacity 2s;
}
figure#lightbox.closed {
    opacity: 0;
    transform: scale(0) translate(-50%, -50%);
}
figure#lightbox.open {
    opacity: 1;
    transform: scale(1) translate(-50%, -50%);
}
```

When the figure is closed, its opacity is set to 0. The figure is also scaled down to nothing. The result is that you can't see anything

If the figure is open, the opacity and scale will change to normal visibility and normal scale. The special effect, however, is in the transition property.

In CSS, transition basically means change slowly. In this case, the opacity changes over one second, to produce a fade-in effect. The scale increases over two seconds, but not evenly, due to the cubic-bezier value.

To allow CSS to do its job, we'll make two changes. First, we'll only change the display property of the background, but not the figure:

```
function loadImage() {
    ...

    img.onload = event => {
//  background.style.display = figure.style.display =
        'block';
        background.style.display = 'block';
        ...
    };
}

function show(event) {
    ...
}

function hide(event) {
//  background.style.display = figure.style.display = 'none';
    background.style.display = 'none';
    ...
}
```

The second is to apply the closed or open class to the figure:

```
function loadImage() {
    ...

    img.onload = event => {
    //  background.style.display = figure.style.display =
        'block';
        background.style.display = 'block';
        figure.classList.add('open');
        figure.classList.remove('closed');
    };
}

function show(event) {

    ...

}

function hide(event) {
//  background.style.display = figure.style.display = 'none';
    background.style.display = 'none';
    figure.classList.remove('open');
    figure.classList.add('closed');

    ...

}
```

Normally, you would only need a single class to toggle between two states, as we've done in other projects. However, in this case, this would have involved setting the opacity of the figure to 0, which would interfere with the previous versions of the code.

Moving the Code to the Library

Now that everything's working, you can move the code to the library.

Since all of the code is in a single function, it's easy enough to just cut and paste it into the library.js file. There's already a link to it in the HTML file.

You can add the following block comment:

```
/*  function doLightbox(container)
    ==================================================
    Function to implement lightbox functionality for
    a gallery of images.

    Use the following Structure:

    <div id="...">
        <a href="..."><img src="..." title="..."></a>
        <a href="..."><img src="..." title="..."></a>
        <a href="..."><img src="..." title="..."></a>
    </div>

    The anchors include a reference to the larger image.
    The images include a thumbnail of the image.
    ================================================== */
```

Revisiting the Slide Show

In Chapter 4, we developed a simple slide show. It does the job, but it lacks some of the pizzazz we added to the lightbox gallery in this chapter.

In this section, we're going to add some fading effects to the slide show.

To begin with, we'll need to reopen the slideshow.html, slideshow.js, and library.js files.

Fading the Image with CSS

To fade each image in, we will transition the opacity of the element, which is how transparent the element is. An opacity of 0 is completely transparent; hence, it is invisible; an opacity of 1 is solid. Transitioning the opacity value from 0 to 1 will fade the element in.

To begin with, we'll add a style sheet and a few rules, as we did for the lightbox gallery:

```
function doSlides(images, containerSelector, delay=3000) {

    ...

    // Fading
        let style = document.createElement('style');
        document.head.insertAdjacentElement('afterbegin',
        style);

        style.sheet.insertRule(`
            div#slides>img {
                opacity: 0;
            }
        `);
        style.sheet.insertRule(`
            div#slides>img.showing {
                transition: opacity 1s;
                opacity: 1;
            }
        `);

    function toggle() {
        ...
    }
    ...
}
```

The initial opacity of the image will be 0, which means it is transparent. We transition that to 1, which will be solid. The transition will take one second.

CSS transitions only run when you change the state of the element. In this case, we will change the class, which will be showing.

Triggering the Transition

We'll change the state in the next() function:

```
function next() {
    // Populate Image
        img.src = `images/slides/${images[slideNumber].src}`;

        img.classList.add('showing');

        caption.textContent = images[slideNumber]. caption;
        img.title = images[slideNumber].caption;
        img.alt = images[slideNumber].caption;
        slideNumber++;

    ...
}
```

However, if the class has already been added, adding it again has no effect, and the transition won't be triggered. You'll have to remove it first:

```
function next() {
    // Populate Image
        img.src = `images/slides/${images[slideNumber].src}`;

        img.classList.remove('showing');
        img.classList.add('showing');

    ...
}
```

This still won't work, because the browser will take a shortcut to save unnecessary extra work. If you're going to remove a class and add it again, the browser decides to do nothing, so the transition *still* won't be triggered. However, if we can trick the browser into updating the document *between* those two statements, it will need to remove and then add the class as required, and so the transition will be triggered.

One way to force an update is to read the size of an element. Since size *may* be affected by CSS, the browser will have to apply the change to the class before measuring the element. Then the next change in the class will also be applied:

```
function next() {
    // Populate Image
          img.src = `images/slides/${images[slideNumber].src}`;

          img.classList.remove('showing');
          img.offsetHeight;
          img.classList.add('showing');

    ...
}
```

The .offsetHeight property is one of many properties that give the current size of an element. Since .offsetHeight can be affected by CSS, the browser will need to make any adjustments as instructed before reading it.

JavaScript will happily allow you to use any expression as a statement, such as 1+2;, and we've seen that in the use strict statement at the beginning. For the most part, the value is ignored, since you don't actually do anything with it. Sometimes, you will see it written with the void operator:

```
img.classList.remove('showing');
void img.offsetHeight;
img.classList.add('showing');
```

The void operator will always result in undefined, which can be useful if you don't have any stray values lying around in your code.

This trick of reading a property between class changes to force the browser to act is the key to getting CSS transitions working in JavaScript.

Cross Fading

The only problem with the fade in previously is that every new image starts blank: that's the flash you see when the image changes. If you want to fade from one image to the next, that is called **cross fading**.

To implement a cross fade, you'll need an extra img element, sitting over the original, so you can fade from one to the other. You'll see the process in Figures 9-3 to 9-5. Using the extra image:

- Set its opacity to 1, making it solid. Then, copy the old image to the extra image in front.

Figure 9-3. *Both images are solid*

- Populate the original img element with the new image. You won't be able to see it yet, because it's behind the other.

Figure 9-4. *New image has changed*

- Trigger a CSS transition to set the front opacity to 0, making it invisible.

Figure 9-5. *Front image fading out*

That's the process. We'll now create the additional image.

Creating the Extra Image

We'll create the extra image by copying the original img element. This is called cloning the element. This way, we make sure that the new image has the same dimensions as the original.

To clone an element, use cloneNode(). Technically all elements in a document are called **nodes** to reflect their position in the Document Object Model. We'll also give it an id to be used later:

```
function doSlides(images, containerSelector, delay=3000) {
    //  Elements
        let container = document.querySelector(container
        Selector);
        let img = container.querySelector('img');
        let prefetch = new Image();

    // Cross Fade
        let crossFade = img.cloneNode();
        crossFade.id = 'crossfade';
        img.insertAdjacentElement('afterend', crossFade);

    ...
}
```

The new img element is inserted immediately after the original so that it will be displayed after.

Styling the New Image

If you view your document, you will see a big space below the original image. The CSS style sheet does have the styling needed to position the new image over the other. We'll add that to the code the way we did for the fading effect.

At the same time, we can remove the old CSS rules so that they don't interfere with this version.

```
style.sheet.insertRule(`
    div#slidese {
        position: relative;
    }
`);
 style.sheet.insertRule(`
   div#slides>img#crossfade {
        display: block;
        position: absolute;
        top: 0; left: 0;
        opacity: 1;
   }
`);
style.sheet.insertRule(`
   div#slides>img#crossfade.fading {
        transition: opacity 2500ms;
        opacity: 0;
   }
`);
```

Here, we'll leave the original image alone and let the new crossFade image do all of the hard work. Apart from the opacity and transition properties:

- Images, by default, display inline, like text. We need to change that to block so that we have more control over its size and position.

- position: absolute; means that we can position it anywhere we like relative to its container, which is the parent div. We want it positioned at top: 0; left: 0;, which is at the top left corner.

- If you're wondering, top left corner of what? The
  position: relative; property for the div answers
  that: it will be the corner of its container.

Triggering the Cross Fade

To actually get the cross fading going, the first thing to do is to copy the old
image into the cross fade image:

```
function next() {
    // Copy to Cross Fade
        crossFade.src = img.src;
        crossFade.alt = img.alt;

    ...

}
```

Technically every image should include an alt attribute, so we just
copy it from the original.

The next image will be assigned as before, but now we change the class
of the cross fade image, not the original:

```
function next() {
    crossFade.src = img.src;
    img.src = `images/slides/${images[slideNumber].src}`;

    // img.classList.remove('showing');
    // img.offsetHeight;
    // img.classList.add('showing');

    crossFade.classList.remove('fading');
    crossFade.offsetHeight;
    crossFade.classList.add('fading');

    ...

}
```

Again the previous code has been commented out because you won't need it anymore. Normally, you would expect to delete unwanted code, but we have left it here in the form of comments so that you can compare the two techniques. You might even decide that you prefer it the old way.

Summary

In this project, we developed a lightbox utility to pop up larger images from smaller thumbnails. We also applied these techniques to enhancing the slide show from Chapter 4.

Hijacking Anchors

The thumbnails for the slide show are contained in HTML anchors that reference the larger version. We can intercept these anchors by applying a `click` event listener to the anchor and stopping the default behavior.

Both the anchor and the nested image contain useful data in addition to the image itself: the anchor has the reference to the larger image, and the image has a `title` attribute that we can use as a caption.

When you click on an image in an anchor, both the image and the anchor experience the `click` event. To extract the right data from the right element, we distinguish between `target`, which refers to the image clicked on, and `currentTarget`, which refers to the containing anchor.

Adding Elements and Styles

In order to manage the lightbox, it's better to create the supporting elements so that the original HTML doesn't need too much accommodating.

The same can be said for additional styles for the new elements. It's possible to create a style block and add it to the head section of the web page. It's best to add it to the beginning so that external style sheets can be applied afterward.

The new style block should contain just enough CSS for the effect to work. This includes setting the background to cover the screen translucently and the CSS to allow the popup to appear in the center of the screen. An additional style sheet can handle the cosmetic aspects.

Showing and Hiding Content

Content visibility can be manipulated by changing the display property of elements. For more effect, the class property of the elements can be manipulated so that the CSS styles can handle hiding and showing.

Changing the class is particularly useful if we want the showing and hiding to be more interesting, such as zooming in the lightbox gallery and fading in the slide show.

A transition can be triggered by changing the class of an element and changing it again. However, because JavaScript tends to consolidate changes, the browser must be forced to update the screen by reading an affected property, such as the .offsetHeight property.

Timing

Since images are loaded as a separate resource, they are always loaded asynchronously. This creates a problem when relying on an image that hasn't yet loaded.

The onload event can be used to trigger wait until an image has loaded before attempting to use it.

Using the Keyboard

It's possible to use the keyboard to manipulate the gallery. By adding a keyboard event listener, we can respond to certain keys to move through the gallery.

Refactoring

Refactoring refers to changing the code so that it behaves in the same way but is more adaptable. This is particularly important when trying to reuse code that had limited application during its development.

Parent, Child, and Sibling Elements

When navigating through a collection of elements, we need to be aware of the methods for referencing nearby elements.

Adjacent elements may be referenced as previous or next siblings. The first and last elements in the collection must be referenced as the first and last children of their parent element.

Cross Fade

Although implementing a fade is simple, by changing a class to trigger a transition, creating a cross fade requires additional work.

To create a cross fade, we can clone the existing image and use CSS to position it over the original. The original image is then copied into the cross fade image, and the original image is replaced. The cross fade is effected by fading out the cross fade image, allowing the new image to show through.

Coming Up

The lightbox utility we developed here can be used with any gallery project. However, it does require that you have prepared a div container with a collection of anchors and images, and so it is not quite as convenient or as flexible as it might be.

To make using the lightbox simpler, we can instead have a CSV file with image file names and captions. Then JavaScript can read the file and generate the anchors and images for us. It would also be easier to make changes without the inconvenience of toying with the HTML.

The same would apply to the slide show, where we could fetch a list of images and use that to populate the slide show.

To fetch more data from the web server requires a technique called Ajax. Ajax allows JavaScript to request and receive additional data. This data may be simple text, or it may be more complex. We can then use the data to make changes to the current page.

In the next chapter, we will look at an introduction to Ajax and how we can use it to load additional content from the web server.

CHAPTER 10

Project: An Introduction to Ajax

If you're trying to run this project without a web server, you're probably out of luck. JavaScript cannot make Ajax requests to different domains unless the other domain specifically allows this. This is called the **Same-Origin Policy**.

Modern browsers tend to regard different documents opened locally (via File: Open ...) as coming from different domains, *even if they're in the same folder.* As a result the Ajax requests will be denied. Files fetched from the same location using the `http://` protocol are regarded as from same origin, which is why you'll need a web server for this chapter.

The only part of this project that will work is the last section, since it specifically accesses a different web server. You don't need a heavy-duty web server to run this project. You can use a light-duty one from `https://github.com/manngo/micro-web-server/releases/latest`.

© Mark Simon 2023
M. Simon, *JavaScript for Web Developers*, https://doi.org/10.1007/978-1-4842-9774-2_10

In some of the projects so far, there was a lot of static content. The slide show uses a hard-coded list of images. The project on showing and hiding content manipulated existing content on the page. And the lightbox project required a collection of thumbnail images and links.

Classically, when you load a page from the web server, complete with images, CSS files, and other associated resources, the connection is closed and the browser deals with what it has got. With JavaScript, however, you can fetch additional resources using a process referred to as **Ajax**.

Ajax is a term apparently coined by James Garrett to describe a collection of technologies that allow the browser to interact with the server without having to reload everything from scratch.

In our case, we'll use JavaScript to establish another connection with the same or a different web server, allowing it to request additional resources or send information back to the server.

You have already seen a simple form of the idea in the slide show project. Every time you change the image's `.src` property, you establish a new connection with the server to get another image. In a primitive way, you are also communicating back to the server in that each request for an image can be processed and possibly logged.

Modern JavaScript now has the ability to do this in a much more sophisticated way, with live updating both at the server end and at the browser end.

Modern Ajax was first implemented using a special `XMLHTTPRequest` object, which was later improved to add more features. This is still available but can be tricky to implement.

Today all modern browsers implement the Fetch API, which allows you to use the `fetch` function to do most of the hard work. It's much simpler than the older `XMLHTTPRequest` object.

In this chapter, we'll explore Ajax in a number of minor projects. Each one will use Ajax to fetch additional data from the server.

- The first section uses hijacked links to fetch additional HTML content.

- The second section implements a slide show by fetching a list of images from the server and using the code you've already written to run the slide show.

- The third section does something similar with a lightbox gallery. In addition, we'll create the elements that contain the thumbnail images.

- The fourth section fetches a list of countries from a server to generate a menu. We then use the menu to refresh a form with more data fetched from the server.

In doing this, we'll develop skills in

- Understanding asynchronous processing

- Using the fetch() function to get data from a server

- Working the JSON string data format to transfer complex data

- Creating elements on the web page

- Working with an Ajax API to access a data service

We'll need to open ajax.html to see what's going on and ajax.js to write the code. We'll also use existing code from the library.js file.

Timing Problems

In the following discussion, make sure that you have a page open, such as the `ajax.html` page.

If you don't have a page open, you're likely to run into Content Security Policy errors.

The hardest thing about working with Ajax has always been a matter of timing. All communication with the web server takes time, and JavaScript doesn't like to be kept waiting.

Take, for example, the following code:

» `var image = new Image;`
» `image.src = 'https://pure-javascript.net/random.jpg';`
» `console.log(image.width);`

The `Image` object is a virtual image that will have the properties of an image but won't actually be displayed.

If you run this once, you'll probably get a result of 0. If you run it again, you'll possibly get a more meaningful value, but not necessarily.

The problem occurs because request for the new image takes a little while. JavaScript, not wishing to hang around, goes on to the next line and attempts to read the width of the image before it's available, giving a result of 0.

We say that the image is loaded **asynchronously**, that is, in the background.

To save you further waiting, the image is probably stored in the browser cache, so next time it should load more quickly – possibly quickly enough for JavaScript to be able to examine its width, which is why you might get a nonzero result if you try it again.

One way to get JavaScript to wait for the image is to use a **callback** function:

```
»   var image = new Image;
»   image.onload=function(event) {
        console.log(image.width);
    };
»   image.src = 'https://pure-javascript.net/random.jpg';
```

The image's `onload` property is supplied a function that will run once the image has finished loading. This now works as expected by deferring acting on the image.

When using Ajax, you will constantly run into similar timing problems: you are trying to fetch a resource, such as text, but JavaScript is impatient to carry on, so the data always arrives too late. The classic way to handle asynchronous Ajax calls was also to use an `onload` event listener to defer further processing to a callback function. With Ajax, however, callback functions are much more complicated, particularly if you need to make another Ajax call after that.

Modern JavaScript has addressed this problem with **promises**. A promise allows you to include code that will run when it's ready without all the mucking about with callbacks.

Using Fetch

The `fetch()` function requests some data from a server and returns a **promise**. A promise is a special object that allows you to add what happens next, similar to adding a series of callback functions.

A typical pattern is

```
//  Hypothetical Example
    fetch(url)                      //  Step 1: Request Something
    .then(processResponse)          //  Step 2
    .then(processData);             //  Step 3
```

The url is where you expect to find the data. Each successive step is a function that is sent to the .next() method. The function data will depend on what's happened in the previous step. Here, we've used the names processResponse and processData, though you would very often use function expressions instead.

For the fetch() function, the next step will get a **response** object as its parameter, typically, though not necessarily, referred to as response. The response object contains all sorts of details returned from the server, but we're usually interested in extracting the data.

You can define the processResponse() function like this:

```
function processResponse(response) {
    return response.text();
}
```

The .text() method extracts the text from response. The result isn't actually just the text: it's another promise object with the text. In later sections, we'll also use a json() method, once we find out what that means.

We can, of course, use an arrow function expression for this:

```
response => {
    return response.text();
}
```

If all you're doing is returning a single value, there's an even shorter form of the arrow function expression:

```
response => response.text();
```

The fetch() function can now look like this:

```
//  Still a Hypothetical Example
fetch(url)
.then(response => response.text())
.then(processData);
```

The next step will involve the actual data. The processData function will get a single parameter with the text from the previous step. Again, we can use an arrow function expression if the processing is simple enough:

```
//  Still still a Hypothetical Example
fetch(url)
.then(response => response.text())
.then(test => {
    console.log(text);
});
```

This arrow function is doing more than just returning a value, which is why the code is inside braces.

We can try this out in the console:

```
»   fetch('https://pure-javascript.net/quote.txt')
.then(response => response.text())
.then(text => {
    console.log(text);
});
```

After a brief pause, you'll get a random quotation from Groucho Marx, such as

I've been looking for a girl like you – not you, but a girl like you.

That's the principle. Now we'll put this into practice. For the project, we'll need work with the files ajax.html and ajax.js.

The HTML file has four sections we'll use to work with Ajax. The `ajax.js` file includes the following code:

```
init();

function init() {
    ajaxContent();
    ajaxSlideshow();
    ajaxLightbox();
    ajaxCountries();
}

function ajaxContent() {

}

function ajaxSlideshow() {

}

function ajaxLightbox() {

}

function ajaxCountries() {

}
```

Each of the functions handles one of the sections of HTML.

Fetching Selected Content

In this first part of the project, we will use Ajax to fetch text content in response to clicking on a link. If you open the file `ajax.html`, you will see a set of links inside a list:

```
<ul id="links">
    <li><a href="ajax/aardvark.txt">Spotted Aardvarks</a></li>
    <li><a href="ajax/starry-night.txt">Starry Night</a></li>
    <li><a href="ajax/lucky.txt">The Lucky Country</a></li>
    <li><a href="ajax/australia.txt">Australia</a></li>
</ul>
```

If you click on one of the links, the browser will load with the new text, but we want to hijack the link and have the browser load the content into a container div instead:

```
<div id="content"></div>
```

Clicking on a link should populate the div with the new content. The content itself is a text file, but it actually contains HTML code.

We can set up the preliminary JavaScript in the function ajaxContent():

```
function ajaxContent() {
    let links = document.querySelector('ul#links');
    let content = document.querySelector('div#content');

}
```

The links variable references the list of links, and the content variable references the div that will be populated.

Hijacking the Links

We have gone through the process of hijacking links before in the lightbox project. In this case, we'll take a different approach and use a delegated event listener – that is, we'll put the event listener on the container.

We begin by putting the event listener on the onclick property of the links container:

```
function ajaxContent() {
    let links = document.querySelector('ul#links');
    let content = document.querySelector('div#content');

    links.onclick = event => {
        event.preventDefault();

    }
}
```

We've also included event.preventDefault() to stop the links from loading a new page.

Fetching the Content

From here, we can simply load the content using the fetch() function, in a similar way to the fetch exercise before. Since the anchors already have a reference to the content, we can use that in the URL parameter:

```
function ajaxContent() {
    let links = document.querySelector('ul#links');
    let content = document.querySelector('div#content');

    links.onclick = event => {
        event.preventDefault();

        fetch(event.target.href)
        .then(response => response.text())
        .then(text => {
            content.innerHTML = text;
        });
    }
}
```

It's important to remember to use event.target here. Even though the event listener is on the containing list, the event.target references the element you actually clicked on: the anchor. From the anchor, we can use the .href property that is the URL of the content.

As with the previous exercise, we begin by fetching the text from the response and go on to process it in the next step. In this case, it's just a case of filling in the content div using its innerHTML.

We can now put this to the test by reloading the page and clicking on the four links.

One of the benefits of this technique is that you can make changes to the content to be loaded without tampering with the HTML file itself.

An Ajax Slide Show

The next section of the project revisits the slide show.

In the slide show project, the images to be loaded were hard-coded, first as an array of image file names, then as an array of objects with the image file name and a caption. What we will do now is to load this collection from an external source using Ajax.

In the ajax.html file, there are only a few lines of code for the slide show:

```
<div id="slides">
    <img width="640" height="480" src="" title="Missing Image"
        alt="Missing Image">
</div>
```

That's all there really is in the slideshow.html file as well.

Most of the hard work is done in the doSlides() function in the library file. What we'll do here is fetch the array of slide objects using Ajax.

But first, we'll need to learn a little about a data format called JSON.

An Introduction to JSON

Traditionally simple data can be stored and transmitted as a text file. That's no good for more complex data structures. One alternative is to structure the text file using XML, which is a markup language, similar to HTML. That's where the **X** in Ajax is supposed to come from: Asynchronous JavaScript and XML.

XML is very popular but has proved to be over the top in JavaScript applications. Instead, a simpler and more direct file format has been developed.

You have already seen that you create an object using the following JavaScript:

```
»   var apple = {
        name: 'Granny Smith',
        shape: 'Round',
        colour: 'Green'
    };
```

You can also create an array of objects using the following:

```
»   var apples = [
        { name: 'Granny Smith', shape: 'Round', colour:
        'Green' },
        { name: 'Fuji', shape: 'Round', colour: 'Red' },
    ];
```

Of course, the spacing and indentation are optional. It's only there to make it easier to read for humans.

Note the comma after the last item. That's probably a little careless, but JavaScript will forgive that and politely ignore it.

The preceding code is pure JavaScript. JSON extends this notation to strings. The word JSON is pronounced "j-son" and means **JavaScript Object Notation**. The string form is very similar to an object literal, but it does impose some very strict requirements. A JSON version of the second example would be

```
»   var apples = `[
        {"name":"Granny Smith", "shape":"Round",
        "colour":"Green"},
        {"name":"Fuji", "shape":"Round", "colour":"Red"}
    ]`;
```

Notice that the string is enclosed in backticks. That's not necessary in JSON, of course, but it allows us to write the string on multiple lines.

The string is very similar to the array of objects previously, but notice the notational differences:

- Each property name is enclosed in double quotes.

- All strings are enclosed in double quotes, *not* single quotes.

- There cannot be a trailing comma after the last item.

This would also be valid for a normal JavaScript object literal but is an absolute requirement for JSON.

Once you have the JSON text, you can normally convert it to a proper JavaScript using `JSON.parse(...)`:

```
»   var apples = `[
        {"name":"Granny Smith", "shape":"Round",
        "colour":"Green"},
        {"name":"Fuji", "shape":"Round", "colour":"Red"}
    ]`;
    apples = JSON.parse(apples);
```

The `JSON` built-in object has just two methods: `JSON.parse()` converts a string to an object, and `JSON.stringify()` does the reverse.

If you're wondering why you would bother with converting between strings and object data, it's because strings are an easy, safe form of data – they're easily transmitted over an Internet connection and easily saved in a text file. By devising a way to encode objects in a string, you can store or transmit more complex data.

JSON has become so popular that it's widely supported in all sorts of other platforms where there's no JavaScript in sight. For example, PHP, Python, and some databases also support the JSON format.

Loading the Slides File

There is a file in the `images/slides/` directory called `slides.json`. We're going to fetch that file in the same way that we fetched the text content in the previous section.

The following will eventually be added to the ajaxSlides() function, but we'll first experiment with it in the console.

We can take the data and use the `JSON.parse()` function to interpret it. Remember to have the page `ajax.html` open when you try this to avoid Cross Origin errors:

```
»   fetch('images/slides/slides.json')
    .then(response => response.text())
    .then(text => {
        let data = JSON.parse(text);
        console.log(data);
    });
```

That would work, but the response object also has a convenient shortcut method called `.json()` that will do that for us:

```
»   fetch('images/slides/slides.json')
    .then(response => response.json())
    .then(data => {
```

```
    console.log(data);
});
```

We can now build that in our code.

The function to manage the slide show is called ajaxSlides():

```
function ajaxSlideshow() {

}
```

In the function, we can fetch the JSON file and process it:

```
function ajaxSlideshow() {
    fetch('images/slides/slides.json')
    .then(response => response.json())
    .then(data => {

    });
}
```

There's only one more step.

Running the Slide Show

All of the hard work is actually complete. Recall that we've saved a function in the library file called doSlides():

```
doSlides(images, containerSelector, delay)
```

In this case, the images object will come from the fetch() function, and the containerSelector is just the reference to the div in the HTML:

```
function ajaxSlideshow() {
    fetch('images/slides/slides.json')
    .then(response => response.json())
    .then(data => {
```

```
    doSlides(data, 'div#slides', 3000);
  });
}
```

The delay is set to the default 3000, but you can change it to anything you like, especially for testing.

An Ajax Lightbox Gallery

For the Ajax slide show, the only thing that was seriously different was the source of the image collection. Previously, the collection was hard-coded in the JavaScript code. Using Ajax, you can get the collection from a loaded file.

In the lightbox gallery, however, it's a little more complicated. The gallery started off with a collection of images in links in the HTML which we then hijacked to use with the lightbox. In the current document, this is all you'll find:

```
<div id="catalogue"></div>
```

which, you'll agree, isn't very much. We're going to use Ajax, in combination with a little DOM manipulation, to populate the catalogue and then let our library doLightbox() function do the rest.

The JavaScript code will be in the ajaxLightbox() function.

Fetching the Gallery Data

The images in the lightbox gallery are the same as the ones in the slide show. What that means is we can start off in the same way as for the slide show:

```
function ajaxLightbox() {
    fetch('images/slides/slides.json')
```

```
.then(response => response.json())
.then(data => {

});
}
```

From here, the task is to use this data to generate the gallery.

Creating the Gallery Elements

The plan is to add the gallery elements to the container. First, we'll set up a variable to reference the container:

```
function ajaxLightbox() {
    let catalogue = document.querySelector('div#catalogue');
    ...
}
```

Remember that the data from the fetch() function will be an array of objects. We can iterate through this array:

```
function ajaxLightbox() {
    let catalogue = document.querySelector('div#catalogue');

    fetch('images/slides/slides.json')
    .then(response => response.json())
    .then(data => {
        data.forEach(item => {
            // create gallery element
        });
    });
}
```

Each gallery element is an image in an anchor:

```
<a href="..."><img src="..." title="..." alt="..." width="160"
height="120"></a>
```

We'll create these elements and add them to the gallery.

In most of the preceding code, we've used `document.createElement()`
to create an element and add it to a container. However, there is also
the ability to create the element using HTML code and adding it using
`.insertAdjacentHTML()`:

```
// Not Yet
    data.forEach(item => {
        catalogue.insertAdjacentHTML(
            'beforeend',
            `<a href="..."><img src="..." title="..." alt="..."
                width="160" height="120"></a>`
        );
    });
```

The new element is added beforeend, which means it's added to the
end of the container. We've put the HTML string inside backticks because
we'll need the template literal.

For the actual element, there are a lot of values to substitute. However,
we can break up the HTML string over a few lines:

```
data.forEach(item => {
    catalogue.insertAdjacentHTML(
        'beforeend',
        `<a href="images/photos/large/${item.src}">
            <img src="images/photos/small/${item.src}"
                title="${item.caption}" alt="${item.caption}"
                width="160" height="120"
            >
```

```
        </a>`
    );
});
```

You can write it on one line, of course, but it certainly won't fit in this book.

Once you've got the gallery populated, you can send it off to the doLightbox() function:

```
function ajaxLightbox() {
    let catalogue = document.querySelector('div#catalogue');

    //  fetch ...

    doLightbox('div#catalogue');
}
```

The finished function should look like this:

```
function ajaxLightbox() {
    let catalogue = document.querySelector('div#catalogue');
    fetch('images/slides/slides.json')
    .then(response => response.json())
    .then(data => {
        data.forEach(item => {
            catalogue.insertAdjacentHTML(
                'beforeend',
                `<a href="images/photos/large/${item.src}">
                    <img src="images/photos/small/${item.src}"
                        title="${item.caption}"
                        alt="${item.caption}"
                        width="160" height="120"
```

```
                    >
            </a>`
        );
    });
    doLightbox('div#catalogue');
  });
}
```

You'll probably notice that the gallery has more images than in the original version. That's one of the benefits of this technique: the gallery has become more flexible.

Accessing a Database

One of the most powerful applications of Ajax is when the data is dynamic in origin. This typically comes from a database on the server end.

You can't access the database directly using JavaScript. What you can do is make a request to the database server via the web server. The idea is that the web server is expected to be running some sort of application listening for such requests.

You won't be able to try this on the sample site if you're running it in a light web server such as the Micro Web Server. If you happen to be running it through something more powerful, such as XAMPP, or even a full web server, then there's a PHP script that will do the job.

In this section, we'll assume that you're not running such a web server. Instead, we'll rely on an application on the live site.

A service provided for access to Ajax is typically referred to as an API, which is a very dated term. It means an Application Programming Interface. In reality, it just means that it will accept correctly formatted requests and return some sort of result.

In this example, we'll work with an API that supplies some information about countries around the world.

The service we'll be using will return JSON formatted data. That's not always the case. A common alternative format is XML, which JavaScript doesn't handle without a lot of extra work.

Not all APIs are free to use for one and all. Some require registration, and some require money to change hands.

In any case, accessing data on another server isn't always allowed. The server needs to be set up to allow requests from other origins. Those that offer an API will naturally have done that.

Working with the API

The API is typically in the form of a URL with a query string. A query string is the part after the question mark that gives additional information.

When an API is made available, you would expect some instructions as to how to use it. In this case:

- The URL by itself returns a list of countries.

- The query string id=... will return details for a particular country.

In many cases, you also need to prove some sort of key to identify the user.

In the live sample, the URL is

```
https://pure-javascript.net/resources/countries.php
```

You can try this in your browser.

You'll find that the URL by itself returns a JSON string, which is a list of country ids and names.

```
[
    { "id": "af", "name": "Afghanistan" },
    { "id": "al", "name": "Albania" },
    { "id": "dz", "name": "Algeria" },

    ...
    { "id": "zm", "name": "Zambia" },
    { "id": "zw", "name": "Zimbabwe" }
]
```

Your browser may interpret the JSON to give you more of a data-oriented view. You may be able to view the raw data to see the actual JSON string.

You can test the query string by putting it after the URL:

```
https://pure-javascript.net/resources/countries.php?id=au
```

You'll now get the details for one country:

```
{
    "id":"au",
    "name":"Australia",
    "local_name":"Australia",
    "capital":"Canberra",
    "alpha3":"AUS",
    "tld":"au",
    "numeric":"036",
    "phone":"61",
    "continent":"Australia",
    "population":"22751014",
    "area":"7741220",
```

```
    "coastline":"25760",
    "currency":"AUD"
}
```

We won't use all of these details.

Using the API with Ajax

Near the bottom of the sample page is a form that will accommodate some country details. Here is a simplified version of that form:

```
<form id="country-details">
    <table>
        <tbody>
            <tr><th><label>Select Country</label></th>
                <td><select name="id"></select></td>
            </tr>
            <tr><th><label>Local Name</label></th>
                <td><output name="local-name"></td>
            </tr>
            <tr><th><label>TLD</label></th>
                <td><output name="tld"></td>
            </tr>
            <tr><th><label>Continent</label></th>
                <td><output name="continent"></td>
            </tr>
            <tr><th><label>Currency</label></th>
                <td><output name="currency"></td>
            </tr>
        </tbody>
    </table>
</form>
```

The form elements are mostly output elements for the received data. However, the form includes a select element that will appear as a drop-down menu. Currently the select element is empty: we'll need to populate it with JavaScript.

For a normal select element, the items would be option elements:

```
<select name="fruit">
    <option value="a">Apple</option>
    <option value="b">Banana</option>
    <option value="c">Cherry</option>
</select>
```

If the form were to be submitted, the value of the select item would be the value of the selected option.

Preparing the select Element

We'll put all the code in the ajaxCountries() function.

We can begin by locating the form:

```
function ajaxCountries() {
    let countriesForm
        = document.querySelector('form#country-details');
}
```

The problem with drop-down menus is that an item is always selected. It's normally good practice to start with an option that doesn't actually choose anything, something like this:

```
<option value="">Select a Country ...</option>
```

You can create option elements using document.createElement(), but there's a specialized function that simplifies the process:

```
new Option(text, value)
```

Technically Option() is called a constructor function that generates an object; constructors are always used with the new keyword. In this case, the object will be an option element, which is just what we want.

We can append the new option element directly to the select element:

```
function ajaxCountries() {
    let countriesForm
        = document.querySelector('form#country-details');
    countriesForm.elements['id'].append(
        new Option('Select  a Country ...', '')
    );
}
```

Remember, the select element is part of the form, so we can reference it through countriesForm.elements. Here, the text is Select ..., and the value will be an empty string.

The next part will be to fetch the list of countries from the API and use that to populate the rest of the select element.

First, we'll define the URL where we're getting the data from:

```
function ajaxCountries() {
    let url = 'https://pure-javascript.net/resources/
    countries.php';
    ...
}
```

That will simplify the code later when we come to use it.

Next, we can fetch the list of countries from the URL:

```
function ajaxCountries() {
    let url = 'https://pure-javascript.net/resources/
    countries.php';
    let countriesForm
        = document.querySelector('form#country-details');
```

```
countriesForm.elements['id'].append(
    new Option('Select  a Country ...', '')
);

fetch(url)
.then(response => response.json())
.then(data => {
    // Add options
});
}
```

The fetch() function will fetch a JSON object with the list of country ids and names, which we'll turn into option elements.

We can iterate through the data array and use new Option() to add the option elements. The text will be the name property of each item, while the value will be the id property:

```
function ajaxCountries() {
    ...

    fetch(url)
    .then(response => response.json())
    .then(data => {
        data.forEach(item=> {
            countriesForm.elements['id'].append(
                new Option(item.name, item.id));
        });
    });
}
```

If you try this now, you'll see the drop-down menu populated with the list of countries.

The next part will be to populate the rest of the form when you select a country from the menu.

Acting on a Selection

Form elements can have a change in value, and when they do, they trigger a change event. That's another reason why the menu should start with an empty value: this means that there'll always be a change event, even for the first real value.

You can add the event listener simply by assigning the .onchange event property:

```
function ajaxCountries() {
    ...

    countriesForm.onchange = event => {

    };
}
```

On change, there will be another fetch using the current value of the drop-down menu:

```
function ajaxCountries() {
    ...

    countriesForm.onchange = event => {
        fetch(`${url}?id=${event.target.value}`)
        .then(response => response.json())
        .then(data => {
            // process results
        });
    };
}
```

Note that we've put the string into a template literal so that we can use the url variable as well as event.target.value.

The query string is constructed from the string ?id= and the current value of the selected country item.

When we have the results from the fetch() function, we can populate the rest of the form:

```
function ajaxCountries() {
    ...

    countriesForm.onchange = event => {
        fetch(`${url}?id=${event.target.value}`)
        .then(response => response.json())
        .then(data => {
            countriesForm.elements['local-name'].value
                = data['local_name'];
            countriesForm.elements['tld'].value = data['tld'];
            countriesForm.elements['continent'].value
                = data['continent'];
            countriesForm.elements['currency'].value
                = data['currency'];
        });
    }
}
```

Again we use response.json() to convert the received JSON string into an object. Once we have that, we fill in the four output element values.

There's one more task we need to finish the job. At some point, somebody's going to select the first item, Select .... As a developer, you'll need to be aware of the potential errors and try to get to them before the user does.

Remember that the first item is an empty string. When we get the result back from the server, there won't be any data. We can test for that with the nullish coalescing operator (??):

```
function ajaxCountries() {
    ...

    countriesForm.onchange = event => {
        ...
        .then(data => {
            countriesForm.elements['local-name'].value
                = data['local_name'] ?? '';
            countriesForm.elements['tld'].value
                = data['tld'] ?? '';
            countriesForm.elements['continent'].value
                = data['continent'] ?? '';
            countriesForm.elements['currency'].value
                = data['currency'] ?? '';
        });
    }
}
```

The missing data value would be undefined. Using the nullish coalescing operator, we can replace it with an empty string ' '.

The finished code would look like this:

```
function ajaxCountries() {
    let url = 'https://pure-javascript.net/resources/
                countries.php';
    let countriesForm
        = document.querySelector('form#country-details');
    countriesForm.elements['id'].append(new Option('Select
...',''));

    fetch(url)
    .then(response => response.json())
    .then(data => {
```

```
        data.forEach(item=> {
            countriesForm.elements['id'].append(
                new Option(item.name,item.id));
        });
    });

    countriesForm.onchange = event => {
        fetch(`${url}?id=${event.target.value}`)
        .then(response => response.json())
        .then(data => {
            countriesForm.elements['local-name'].value
                = data['local_name'] ?? '';
            countriesForm.elements['tld'].value
                = data['tld'] ?? '';
            countriesForm.elements['continent'].value
                = data['continent'] ?? '';
            countriesForm.elements['currency'].value
                = data['currency'] ?? '';
        });
    }
}
```

Before Ajax and the Ajax functions became a standard part of JavaScript, fetching new data from the server would require reloading a page full of data, which creates an annoying experience for the user.

Summary

In this chapter, we had a look at using Ajax to fetch additional data from the web server. We had already fetched additional data in the form of images in the slide show and lightbox gallery. Here, we looked at fetching text and more complex data.

366

Using the fetch( ) Function

The main problem to overcome is one of timing. Because web requests, including Ajax requests, take some time, the code needs to be written so that processing of the data is deferred until after the data arrives.

The fetch() function allows you to send an Ajax request to the server and returns a Promise object. The Promise object can attach code to process the data after it arrives.

A simple fetch() application can work with two steps after requesting the data: the first is to extract the data from the response, and the second is to process the extracted data.

If the data is a simple text, it can be used immediately, such as for populating the contents of other elements.

Using JSON

JavaScript supports an object literal format that allows you to define an object or an array of objects directly in code.

The JSON string format is a string that resembles an object literal and can be converted to a real object or array of objects using built-in JavaScript functions. The real benefit of JSON is to be able to represent complex data as a single string. A string is easily saved in a text file or transmitted over the Internet, whereas complex data is not so readily managed.

The JSON data can come from a saved file on the server, but it can also be generated dynamically on the server through some server-side processing, such as with PHP and a database.

JavaScript has a built-in function, JSON.parse(), which will convert JSON strings. However, the fetch() response has its own method, .json(), which can do the same with JSON strings received.

Interacting with the DOM

Previous projects interacted with the DOM in either changing or adding elements. In this project, we extended this by populating an element with `.innerHTML`, creating anchors and images for the lightbox gallery with `.insertAdjacentHTML()`, and populating a `select` element with `new Option()`.

We also looked at responding to a form with the `change` event to trigger another `fetch()` and populate the rest of the form.

Ajax APIs

There are many third parties that offer a data service in the form of Ajax APIs. These services often return a JSON string, though some use other forms of data, such as XML.

Accessing a third-party API requires the other server to accept connections. Some will restrict access to registered, and possibly paying, users.

APPENDIX A

Running a Web Server

Although you can run most of the projects by loading the HTML files directly in the browser, you'll come across a few problems that way:

- The `crossorigin` attribute in the `<script>` tag will cause errors. For that reason, it's been commented out in the sample files.

- Ajax won't work.

- You can't use absolute URL paths (starting with the slash /).

To get the fullest experience, it's better to run your project through a web server.

Many web developers have already installed either XAMPP or MAMP, or something like them. They are full web servers, complete with PHP and a database, and possibly a few other services.

If you don't have one installed, you can use a much lighter web server for developing your JavaScript (and HTML and CSS for that matter).

The simplest solution is to download one called Micro Web Server from

`https://github.com/manngo/micro-web-server`

It looks like this:

© Mark Simon 2023
M. Simon, *JavaScript for Web Developers*, https://doi.org/10.1007/978-1-4842-9774-2

Macintosh   **Windows**

To set it up:

1. Select the location of your sample folder.

2. Save the project. You can use **Save As ...** to give your
    project a new name.

3. Check the port number. 8000 is probably OK, but
    8080 is a common alternative.

4. Start.

When the server is started, you'll see a link to the site, something like

`http://localhost:8000`

You can click on it to load the page in your browser.

Alternatively, if you have any of the following packages already
installed, you can set up your own web server.

PHP

PHP can implement a simple web server from the command line. You can
get the details from `www.php.net/manual/en/features.commandline.`
`webserver.php`.

```
cd wherever
php -S localhost:8000
```

370

Python

Python also has a built-in web server that can be run from the command line. You can get the full details at `https://docs.python.org/3/library/http.server.html`.

```
cd wherever
python3 -m httpd.server
```

Node.js

Node.js doesn't have a simple one-liner, but there are a few that are ready to go. Here are two you might like to try:

- GitHub – http-party/http-server: A simple zero-configuration command-line http server

  `https://github.com/http-party/http-server`

- GitHub – tapio/live-server: A simple development http server with live reload capability

  `https://github.com/tapio/live-server`

Pulsar or VSCodium

Both Pulsar and VSCodium (or VSCode if you prefer) have extension packages that will allow you to run your project as a web server.

- Pulsar: atom-live-server (remember, Pulsar is the reincarnation of Atom)

  `https://web.pulsar-edit.dev/packages/atom-live-server`

It's easier to install this from Pulsar's Packages settings.

- VSCodium (VSCode): Live Server – Open VSX Registry

  `https://open-vsx.org/extension/ritwickdey/LiveServer`

  It's easier to install this from the Extension settings.

APPENDIX B

Deferring Scripts

There are two main methods for adding JavaScript to your web page. First, you can add the script in the page itself using a `<script>` tag.

The second method is to add a reference to an external file:

```
<head>
    ...
    <script src="..."></script>
    ...
```

The `src` attribute references the file. The rest of the element is empty – if you add code inside, it will be ignored. The reference is normally in the head element.

You can get a problem with the way the browser loads the script. First, when the browser gets to the script reference, it then pauses rendering the page while it fetches the script. This is different to how it loads an image, which it does in the background.

Second, the browser pauses again while it executes the script. Not only does this interfere with rendering the page, it can also result in errors. It's likely that the JavaScript references part of the page that hasn't loaded or been rendered yet, so all of that will fail.

Modern browsers have solved this problem with two keywords: `async` and `defer`. The `async` keyword will solve the first problem in loading the script in the background while it's working on the HTML. However, it will still pause the rendering while it then processes the HTML. It doesn't solve the problem of referencing parts of the page that aren't there yet.

© Mark Simon 2023
M. Simon, *JavaScript for Web Developers*, https://doi.org/10.1007/978-1-4842-9774-2

The `defer` keyword acts like `async` in that it loads the script in the background. However, it then waits until the browser has finished with the HTML before it executes, thus solving the second problem as well. Figure B-1 describes the process.

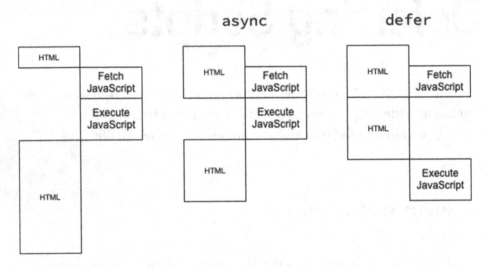

Figure B-1. *Deferring JavaScript*

You would never use both. The `defer` keyword implies `async`.

Older Methods

The `defer` keyword has been available for a very long time, but that doesn't mean that you won't see alternative methods in the wild.

The most common older method is to run the code as an event listener function. The event was typically the `load` event:

```
window.onload = init;

function init() {
    ...
}
```

The load event is triggered when the page has fully loaded, complete with all of the additional resource, such as CSS files and images.

Of course, the function isn't necessarily called init().

You will also see this technique with a function expression:

```
window.onload = function () {
    ...
};
```

This was the dominant technique for many years. You may see it using the addEventListener form:

```
// Using init() function
   window.addEventListener('load', init);

// Using function expression:
   window.addEventListener('load', function() {
      ...
   });
```

For the most part, you don't really need to wait until absolutely everything has finished loading. The document object has an event that is triggered when the content has finished loading, but not necessarily the additional resources:

```
// Using init() function
   document.addEventListener('DOMContentLoaded', init);

// Using function expression:
   document.addEventListener('DOMContentLoaded', function() {
      ...
   });
```

There's nothing technically wrong with these techniques. They're just a lot of extra work when the defer attribute will do the job more efficiently.

There's one additional technique that you'll sometimes see used. Some developers prefer to put the script reference at the end of the HTML to make sure that the browser doesn't see it until last. That was never really necessary, and it starts to interfere with the logical structure of your code.

APPENDIX C

Further Expertise

The only way to really develop expertise is, of course, to just keep writing and to keep reading other developers' code and tips. However, there's also plenty of online help available.

Here are a few places you can go for help:

- MDN Web Docs: `https://developer.mozilla.org/en-US/`

    There's no official JavaScript website, but this site is about as official as you're going to get. It includes some formal descriptions of everything JavaScript, as well as examples and compatibility tables.

    It's not just for Mozilla, either. It's relevant for Chrome, Safari, and Edge too.

- Stack Overflow: `https://stackoverflow.com/`

    If you've searched for answers online before you're likely to have stumbled on to this site. Here, you can register and ask any programming questions and wait for some kind soul to reply.

    Before you start asking questions, however, it's probably a good idea to look at a few other questions to get a feeling for the types of questions that attract helpful responses and the types that attract scorn.

- Can I Use: `https://caniuse.com/`

  This very helpful site is particularly useful if you're trying to see whether a particular new feature is safe to use in today's browsers. It includes additional notes and references to where you can get more details.

Index

A, B

post-increment (a++) operator, 12
addEventListener() function, 141
.addEventListener() method, 235,
    236, 245
addEventListener() method,
    220, 245
Ajax
   accessing database
     API, 357–365
     web server, 356
   CSS files, 338
   fetch, 341–344
   JSON, 367
   lightbox gallery, 352–356
   selected count, 344–346
   slide show, 347–351
   timing problems, 340–341
   XMLHTTPRequest object, 338
alert() function, 43, 72, 91
appendChild() function, 115
Argument, 40
Arithmetic operations/operators, 9
Array, 44
Arrow function, 235
Arrow function expression, 109, 153
Assignment statements, 57

C

callback function, 341
caption property, 162
Cascading Style Sheets (CSS)
   adding HTML, 213–214
   definition, 211
   disabling style, 214–215
   dynamic changes, 229–230
   example, 222, 224
   JavaScript, 213
   properties/classes, 230, 246
   resetting properties, 224–225
   sample file, 212
   storing state, 225–228
   styles property, 223
   transitions, 247
   working, 231–233
Child nodes, 99
Child selector, 105
clearInterval() function, 139
Commenting the
    code out, 21
Comments, 4, 90
   JavaScript interpreter, 20
   nested, 22
   types, 20–21
   uses, 21

© Mark Simon 2023
M. Simon, *JavaScript for Web Developers*, https://doi.org/10.1007/978-1-4842-9774-2